Civic Duty

The Ultimate Guide to the World's
Most Popular Sport Compact Car
— the Honda Civic

Alan Paradise

www.BentleyPublishers.com

table of contents

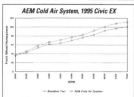

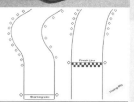

RB | BENTLEY PUBLISHERS | AUTOMOTIVE BOOKS & MANUALS

1734 Massachusetts Avenue   Information that makes
Cambridge, MA 02138 USA   the difference®
800-423-4595 / 617-547-4170
www.**BentleyPublishers**.com

Copies of this book may be purchased from selected booksellers, or directly from the publisher by mail. The publisher encourages comments from the reader of this book. These communications have been and will be considered in the preparation of this and other books. Please write to Bentley Publishers at the address listed on the top of this page.

Since this page cannot legibly accommodate all the copyright notices, the photo credits page listing the source of the photographs or illustrations used constitutes an extension of the copyright page.

Library of Congress Cataloging-in-Publication Data
Paradise, Alan.
    Civic duty : the ultimate guide to the world's most popular sport compact car--the Honda Civic/ Alan Paradise
      p. cm.
    Includes index.
    ISBN 0-8376-0215-7 (alk. paper)
    1. Honda Civic automobile--Customizing. 2. Honda Civic automobile--Performance. I. Title

TL215.H58 P37 2000
629.28'722722--dc21

00-044465

Bentley Stock No. GHCD

03 02 01 00 10 9 8 7 6 5 4 3 2 1

The paper used in this publication is acid free and meets the requirements of the National Standard for Information Sciences-Permanence of Paper for Printed Library Materials. (∞)

Front cover: Photo by Alan Paradise
Back cover: Top two photos courtesy American Honda Motor Co. Bottom two photos by Alan Paradise. Fence image courtesy Photodisc. Captions, top to bottom: 1. *A good club can be your lifeline to optimizing the enjoyment of your Honda.* 2. *This trendy look is inspired by European and American Touring car racing.* 3. *With Honda, size is not a factor—200-300 hp is possible.* 4. *Scallops: classic styling, contemporary design.*

Please read these Warnings and Cautions before proceeding with any maintenance and repair work.

WARNING —

• Do not reuse self-locking nuts or any other fasteners that are fatigued or deformed in normal use. They are designed to be used only once, and become unreliable and may fail when used a second time. This includes, but is not limited to, bolts, washers, self-locking nuts, circlips and cotter pins that secure the subframe, control arms, stabilizer bar, ball joints and other suspension, steering and brake components. Always replace these fasteners with new parts.

• Never work under a lifted vehicle unless it is solidly supported on stands designed for the purpose. Do not support a vehicle on cinder blocks, hollow tiles, or other props that may crumble under continuous load. Do not work under a vehicle that is supported solely by a jack.

• If you are going to work under a vehicle on the ground, make sure that the ground is level. Block the wheels to keep the vehicle from rolling. Never work under the vehicle while the engine is running. Disconnect the battery ground strap to prevent others from starting the vehicle while you are under it.

• Never run the engine unless the work area is well ventilated. Carbon monoxide kills.

• Friction materials such as brake or clutch discs may contain asbestos fibers. Do not create dust by grinding, sanding, or by cleaning with compressed air. Avoid breathing asbestos fibers and asbestos dust. Breathing asbestos can cause serious diseases such as asbestosis or cancer, and may result in death.

• Tie long hair behind your head. Do not wear a necktie, a scarf, loose clothing, or a necklace when you work near machine tools or running engines. If your hair, clothing, or jewelry were to get caught in the machinery, severe injury could result.

• Disconnect the battery ground strap whenever you work on the fuel system or the electrical system. When you work around fuel, do not smoke or work near heaters or other fire hazards. Keep an approved fire extinguisher handy.

• Finger rings should be removed so that they cannot cause electrical shorts, get caught in running machinery, or be crushed by heavy parts.

• Keep sparks, lighted matches, and open flames away from the top of the battery. If hydrogen gas escaping from the cap vents is ignited, it will ignite gas trapped in the cells and cause the battery to explode.

• Catch draining fuel, oil, or brake fluid in suitable containers. Do not use food or beverage containers that might mislead someone into drinking from them. Store flammable fluids away from fire hazards. Wipe up spills at once, but do not store the oily rags, which can ignite and burn spontaneously.

• Some aerosol tire inflators are highly flammable. Use extreme care when repairing a tire that may have been inflated using an aerosol tire inflator. Keep sparks, open flame or other sources of ignition away from the tire repair area. Inflate and deflate the tire at least four times before breaking the bead from the rim. Completely remove the tire from the rim before attempting any repair.

• Do not attempt to work on your vehicle if you do not feel well. You can increase the danger of injury to yourself and others if you are tired, upset or have taken medicine or any other substance that may impair you from being fully alert.

• Some of the vehicles covered by this manual are equipped with a Supplemental Restraint System (SRS) that automatically deploys an airbag in the event of a frontal impact. The airbag unit is an explosive device. Handled improperly or without adequate safeguards, the system can be very dangerous. The SRS system should be serviced only through an authorized Honda dealer.

• Illuminate your work area adequately but safely. A fluorescent worklight is preferable to an incandescent worklight. Use a portable safety light for working inside or under the vehicle. Make sure the bulb is enclosed by a wire cage. The hot filament of an accidentally broken bulb can ignite spilled fuel or oil.

• SRS airbags that have been activated during an accident must always be replaced. Only trained personnel should work on or replace the airbag. Improper installation may result in inadvertent activation or rendering the system useless. The Honda authorized dealer has training, instructions and tools to perform SRS service and repair.

• When driving or riding in an airbag-equipped vehicle, never hold test equipment in your hands or lap while the vehicle is in motion. Objects between you and the airbag can increase the risk of injury in an accident.

• Always observe good workshop practices.Wear goggles when you operate machine tools or work with battery acid. Gloves or other protective clothing should be worn whenever the job requires it.

• Greases, lubricants and other automotive chemicals contain toxic substances, many of which are absorbed directly through the skin. Read manufacturer's instructions and warnings carefully. Use hand and eye protection. Avoid direct skin contact.

CAUTION—

• If you lack the skills, tools and equipment, or a suitable workshop for any procedure described in this book, we suggest you leave such repairs to an authorized Honda dealer or other qualified shop. We especially urge you to consult an authorized Honda dealer before beginning repairs on any vehicle that may still be covered wholly or in part by any of the extensive warranties issued by Honda.

• Honda is constantly improving its vehicles and sometimes these changes, both in parts and specifications, are made applicable to earlier models. Always check with your authorized Honda dealer for the latest parts and service information.

• Before starting a job, make certain that you have all the necessary tools and parts on hand. Read all the instructions thoroughly, do not attempt shortcuts. Use tools appropriate to the work and use only replacement parts meeting Honda specifications. Makeshift tools, parts, and procedures will not make good repairs.

• Use pneumatic and electric tools only to loosen threaded parts and fasteners. Never use these tools to tighten fasteners, especially on light alloy parts.

• Be mindful of the environment and ecology. Before you drain the crankcase, find out the proper way to dispose of the oil. Do not pour oil onto the ground, down a drain, or into a stream, pond, or lake. Consult local ordinances that govern the handling and disposal of chemicals and wastes.

• Before doing any electrical welding on vehicles equipped with the Antilock Braking System (ABS), disconnect the ABS control unit connector.

• Do not quick-charge the battery (for boost starting) for longer than one minute, and do not exceed 15.0 volts at the battery with the boosting cables attached. Wait at least one minute before boosting the battery a second time.

• Honda offers extensive warranties, especially on components of the fuel delivery and emissions control systems. Therefore, before deciding to repair a Honda that may still be covered wholly or in part by any warranties issued by Honda, consult your authorized Honda dealer.

Please also read the Safety Notice and disclaimer on the Copyright page.

To all the early pioneers of import performance who had the courage and insight to bravely step into a new world of speed and beauty. To my wife, Annette, who not only tolerates my automotive obsession, but encourages it. To my son, Cory, who will become part of the next generation of gear heads.

Foreword

By Oscar Jackson

Why the Honda Civic, and is it really an important car? These are questions I get asked quite often. The answer I give is easier than the question. I simply say yes.

Few automobiles in history have had the same lasting effect and influence on the world as the Civic. In fact, the Civic belongs in the same company with the Ford Model T, Volkswagen Beetle and Porsche 911, as one of the cars that have changed the face of how we live, let alone drive.

When the Civic first set down on U.S. soil, hardly a whimper was heard. No big fanfare, no media blitz, no cover of *Motor Trend*. It was just a little, insignificant entry from a Japanese motorcycle manufac-turer…or so we believed. Today, the Civic has become the primary choice for an entirely new generation of hot rodders. The Civic is the '55 Chevy of the import performance world.

What has made the Civic the catalyst for the import performance movement is its simplistic design and universal appeal. Every model can be personalized, modified, made to go fast, look good and deliver years of reliable use. The cars are practical, yet stylish, fun to drive, yet utili-tarian, conservative, and yet innovative. In other words, Honda has accomplished the nearly impossible—designed a car that can be for everyone…from Grandma to street racer.

The evolution of the Civic as an icon of the import performance market started long before the advent of magazines such as *Sport Compact Car* and *Super Street*. In the 1970s, autocrossers began to dis-cover that these front-wheel drive cars could run circles around their

American counterparts (Pinto and Vega). Soon Civic was challenging traditional V8 muscle cars for "fastest time of the day" at many events. The ideal blend of balance and power started turning people on to Honda as a viable alternative to domestic and European marques.

When the first issues of *Sport Compact Car* were produced (1989-90), the Civic was one of the featured models. It soon became evident that the Civic and CRX would dominate the market, thus catapulting the car to star status. The hook, however, was that it remained affordable and accessible.

Enter into the year 2000. Today, the Civic is the most popular car in the import performance niche. From early models to the power potential of the new Si, the Civic, CRX and del Sol are the preferred platforms for speed and beauty.

Building a trick Civic is easier than any other import car. Everything from simple bolt-ons, such as engine dress-up and shift knobs, to performance pistons and superchargers can be installed. Often, the first application that aftermarket companies design and offer is for the Honda Civic. The reason: it's a numbers game. There are so many Civics being built and enjoyed, it makes absolute and perfect sense.

So, when it comes to Honda performance, the Civic nameplate is at the top of the heap. Hey, I should know, I've built a business and reputation concentrating on Honda products. And, while the Accord and Prelude play a part, nothing compares to the interest in the Civic.

As you read through this book, you will find that it is a highly useful guide to everything Civic. There is something for everyone, from the first time builder to the weekend warrior.

You have selected the most popular car in the import performance industry, now it's time to make the most of it.

Preface

By Alan Paradise

Fig. P-1: Honda's Civic has progressed from a humble econobox into a true world-class car. The entire foundation of the import performance interest comes from this model. Contemporary versions feature performance-tuned suspensions, horsepower enhancements, race-influenced styling cues and effective paint schemes.

When automotive experts identify the most significant cars ever created, names like Duesenberg, Rolls Royce, Ferrari, Porsche, Corvette and Mercedes-Benz are generally the subject matter. However, in the annals of automotive history, few makers have had as much of an effect on the market as Honda. Along with Volkswagen, Honda revolutionized the entire industry with cars that fit the times and needs of not just a country but the world.

At the top of the success list for the marques is the first car to break the hold of American iron and become a worldwide icon—the Civic. This book traces the history of the Civic, from its humble beginnings on American roads to its rise to the top of the sales charts. More important, many chapters cover the various facets in which owners can explore the full performance and personalizing potential of Civic coupes and sedans. Included are references to their two-seater brothers—the cult-classic CRX and the open-air, ill-fated del Sol.

Today's Honda performance enthusiast is a multifaceted car owner. The car you race on Sunday, you drive to work on Monday. Thus, you demand a great deal from your subcompact/race car. Reliability is just as important as power. Handling and ride quality need to work together and be equally smooth. Overall appearance is needed for curb appeal, not to mention items such as a comfortable yet sporty interior, an adequate sound system, vehicle protection devices and the ability to pass a smog station without having a heart attack.

In the next 12 chapters you will be exposed to the secrets of suspension performance, quick and easy engine bolt-ons, internal engine performance, drag-racing tips, performance braking, exterior and interior design, graphic treatments for the new millennium, performance driving techniques and, finally, how to get involved with the ever-growing world of events and clubs.

Just a word of warning: as the subtitle implies, the purpose of this book is not to build the ultimate Civic—no one will even achieve that lofty title. This book is about discovering the combination of speed, beauty and reliability that's right for you and your lifestyle. As an enthusiast, I firmly believe in the street scene. I made the mistake of over-building a nice street truck (a 1986 Isuzu) into a trailer queen. After swapping out the four-banger for a TPI engine from a Camaro, unloading the stock rear end for a nine-inch Ford with four-link technology and coil-over shocks, performing massive body modifications, and adding a high-dollar paint job and hundreds of hours on interior upgrades, I was so cautious about driving the truck I nearly developed an ulcer. When not used as a garage fixture, it was trailered to a show, taken off at the event—and back on for home. I hated all that and soon sold the truck for one-third of what it cost to build. I'll never again build or own a vehicle I'm afraid to drive and enjoy.

This belief holds true for a pure race car. Although the idea is ego-lifting, the reality of going from event to event with a garage full of support materials, tools and extra man-power (the wife and kids) brings me back to earth. My family gets more out of a local commute in one of our tricked-out cars than they do sitting around a race track watching the money pit making a few laps or passes—or worst yet, the pride, joy and bank account sitting idle behind poles and rope. Nope, none of that stuff is right for me. I subscribe to the belief "if ya got it, drive it."

It is this philosophy you will find in the following pages. The optimum word is enjoy your Civic. That means nearly everything written in this book is geared for street use. Although some modifications are not street-legal by the California standards book (the basic rulebook of the industry), it doesn't mean you can't do it. It just means you'll need to be aware of the consequences and of how to avoid trouble.

You will also find how-to tips and guides to help make performance and personalizing decisions easier. From suspension spring rates to turbocharging boost factors, we have tried to cover all the bases. Even if you're not looking to build a Mustang-eating Civic, there is plenty of information on basic modifications, interior enhancements and performance driving tips you can use each and every day.

You will notice that a donor car is used as an example in many of the chapters. This 1999 Civic DX is the base model, devoid of

Fig. P-2: Existing for only six model years (1992-97), the del Sol is gaining popularity as a stylish street machine. Although overshadowed by Mazda's Miata and put to rest by the introduction of the BMW Z3, the del Sol offers more performance and styling potential and is considerably easier on the pocketbook.

Fig. P-3: With its roots firmly planted in import performance history, the CRX has become the first true cult car of the sport compact generation. With plenty of aftermarket components readily available, the CRX is an easy entry-level ticket into new-age hot rodding.

power windows, door locks and other luxury items found on the higher-priced EX. The DX gives you an excellent example on which to base your modifications. Ty Tipton, of Tipton Honda in El Cajon, California, donated the car to this cause. Leading aftermarket manufacturers pitched in their support, as you will see along the way.

However, this book is not about a 1999 Civic. It is written to cover all popular models as well as the CRX and del Sol. You will see photos from events such as the NOPI Nationals, NIRA drag racing, Battle of the Imports, Super Street Tour and others. Who knows?—you may even see your car caught on film at one of these events.

One of the wonderful things about a Civic is that it's inexpensive to buy, cheap to operate and easy to modify and personalize. Even on a modest budget, using the tips, techniques, information and sources in this book, anyone can put together a fine example of the first true Japanese icon—the Honda Civic. Enjoy.

The History of the Civic

Fig. 1-1: Until Honda imported the 600 coupe, the Mini Cooper was the tiny tot of American roadways. The product quality and marketing approach propelled Honda past Cooper. Within a few decades every other automaker in the world was forced to chase Honda for automotive world domination.

Who would have believed it? Certainly not Honda. On a brisk morning early in 1969 the first-generation Honda cars were unloaded onto the docks in Long Beach, California. Like shiny little boxes reflecting the sun, a few dozen cars with a strange "H" marker on the short and squared-off deck lid seemed dwarfed next to the larger versions from Toyota and Datsun. Even the Volkswagen Beetle was a large car in comparison to the tiny Honda. No longer were the English Mini Cooper or MG Midget the tiny tots of the great American roadways. Now there was Honda—and little did anyone know, but the U.S. auto market would never be the same.

At the time, domestic automakers were engulfed in muscle car mania. Ford, Chevrolet, Dodge, Plymouth, Pontiac, Oldsmobile and Mercury were locked in a heated battle for the streets. Think about it. By spring of 1970 Ford had the Boss 302 Mustang, Mach One (351 cubic inches), and the Boss 429 (very rare), as well as the Torino. Chevy countered with the Corvette (available with an LT-1 350 or monster 454 V-8), the SS Chevelle (350, 396 or 454), and the most popular muscle car of all, the Camaro (SS350 and SS396, as well as the Z/28—perhaps the best overall performance car of the era). Dodge offered the Charger (383, 440 or 426 HEMI) as well as the Challenger (available with the big blocks as well as the 340 six-pack T/A version). Rounding out the Dodge marque was the little-seen 383- or 440-powered Super Bee and the Dart, with a potent 340 V8. Plymouth's versions were legendary even back then. The 'Cuda was the beast of the boulevard, with an engine choice of either a 383, 440 six-pack or the 426 HEMI—not to mention the AAR, a Trans

From its humble beginnings to how it became the world's most popular sport compact car. Once a car small enough to fit into the trunk of a Cadillac, now it's the model GM wishes they had thought of first.

Am race car with license plates. Pontiac's GTO and Firebird, although overshadowed by Chevrolet's line, had a loyal following. At the same time, Oldsmobile and Mercury mirrored Chevrolet and Ford respectively.

This was the heyday for bigger, more powerful engines. At a mere 25 cents per gallon, gas was cheap, making fuel efficiency a non-issue. The economy was good and life was sweet for everyone with a heavy right foot.

So, as the seasoned longshoremen of Long Beach hooked up the rigging to off-load the boxy little Hondas, more than a few shook their heads in complete disbelief. Little did anyone know that a few years later, the oil-producing countries of the Middle East would deal a death blow to Detroit muscle and send Toyota, Datsun and Honda to the top of the car sales charts. However, as the world stage was being set for Honda dominance, it would take the automaker another decade to establish itself in the same league with Toyota and Nissan (Datsun).

The year 1973 was considered by most automotive journalists as the final year of the true American muscle car. It was early in this historic year that OPEC collaborated to hoard crude oil, sending the industrialized countries of the world to their collective knees. While European countries were already primed for high prices, automakers and car owners here in the United States were spoiled by nearly 30 years of the low prices made pos-

sible by the oil reserves and fossil fuel resources hidden deep within our own soil. We were the richest, most technically advanced society the world had ever seen. In the absence of any real voices about environmental concerns, bigger meant better.

By now you're wondering, why the history lesson? Simple answer—you can't foresee the future without a firm grasp of the past, when Honda was poised to introduce the most sweeping changes in small-car quality and technology.

The foundation for Honda's later success was a diminutive two-seat coupe. These first Hondas to hit the dealers' lots (what few dealers there were) were powered by a tried and true four-stroke Honda motorcycle engine. It produced about 52 horsepower, just enough to send two college-bound students down the highway. The car was like a square box with a small beak. Equipped with miniature 10-inch wheels and pizza-cutter tires, you could park three Hondas in the same space as one Cadillac Sedan de Ville. So light were these first-generation Hondas that if one was parked where you wanted to dock your land yacht, you and three friends could each grab a corner and lift and transplant the tiny Honda to another parking space.

By 1971 there were more Honda dealers, nearly all of them featuring Honda cars as offerings secondary to more established brands. These pioneers would soon be hand-

Fig. 1-2: Here it is, the quiet monster that started it all. This is the first Civic to be imported into the United States. The massive 1,168cc engine produced a neck-snapping 52 horsepower. To say this was tame would be the automotive understatement of the decade, especially when you consider the fact that a Chrysler HEMI V-8 engine could easily produce 52 horsepower per cylinder.

somely rewarded—the second-generation Hondas were now arriving. While still small, the new, aerodynamically designed body reminded people of a two-seater personal spacecraft. With more slope to the nose, a sleek roof line and rear side windows designed in an odd, upsweep shape, the new Honda coupe was sporty. The powerplant was slightly upgraded with a bit more horsepower, and its handling was so nimble and quick that Little Jack Horner would have been envious.

Offered in more vibrant colors, the New Honda N600 Coupe was a slick little car, but, size was still an issue. Toyota's smallest model, the Corolla, was several hundred pounds heavier, offered a real car engine with double the horsepower and could seat four (provided the two passengers in the rear seat were circus contortionists). Still, Honda was building a reputation based on quality and reliability. While Datsun and Toyota owners were getting to know their dealer's service managers, Honda owners were enjoying carefree motoring.

When Honda introduced the Civic, a four-seater in both coupe and sedan versions, the stage was set for a mini-car war among the Japanese Big Three. However, as progressive as Japanese automakers had become, they were still fighting an uphill battle in the import arena with the number one seller, Volkswagen. Volkswagen's history is well documented; its sales were remarkable. So Toyota and Datsun sales and marketing teams set their sights on breaking down the domestic car buyer, and Honda became the beneficiary without having to lift a finger.

When the oil embargo hit, Americans were left with empty tanks in their big, chrome-laden monsters, and the United States was ripe for a Japanese invasion. Within a blink of an eye we Americans surrendered our loyalty to Detroit and scurried to new car dealerships to purchase any car that would deliver a fuel efficiency rating of over 20 miles to the gallon. Nearly overnight Toyota and Datsun dealers sold out of Corollas, Coronas, 510s and small trucks.

Even Mazda, with its radical rotary engine, was selling RX2s faster than they could be imported. It was then, during one of America's darkest times, that Honda shone bright.

By now Honda's Civic was a car superior to its Japanese counterparts. With its German-like quality, it provided more attention to engine and suspension performance than any of its competitors. American consumers, who, just a few years earlier, had been reluctant to even look at a Honda unless it was on two wheels, now converted. As if hearing a tune from a magical piper, people flowed into Honda dealers ready to compare its offerings with Toyota, Datsun and Mazda. When they left their Honda dealer, it was almost always in a new Honda. Ford and General Motors were quickly trying to recover with the Pinto and Vega, but the push was far too little and way too late. The search for the automaker of the future had ended.

In 1975, when the Civic came equipped with the CVCC (compound vortex controlled combustion) engine, the die was cast—this would become the most popular car in the world. But why the Civic? The Toyota Corolla was a more established nameplate, Datsun (now becoming Nissan) had the Sentra with its BMW-like styling, and a handful of slick Mitsubishi products were coming over. The reason was, simply stated, Honda's quality and reliability. Never had consumers seen a car that would run and run without worry. The car's engine seemed bulletproof, while the transmission and transaxle delivered flawless operation. The brakes stopped in plenty of time, and the fit and finish were close to the standards of German cars.

While diehard domestic car lovers discounted the quality of Toyotas, Nissans and Mazdas, Honda products seemed exempt from this criticism. Even the most stubborn of American car loyalists would soon have to eat their words as the quality of U.S.-made cars hit an all-time low. Again, this left Honda to benefit without so much as putting out a marketing effort.

Fig. 1-3: The second generation Honda, the Civic, catapulted Honda into stardom. These coupes and sedans, although they are getting hard to find, make excellent and cost-effective platforms to built a retro sport compact car.

As the Civic progressed and evolved, three versions were offered: a coupe, a sedan and a hatchback coupe. And remember that tiny two-seater with the aerodynamic styling from early 1971? In 1984 it had grown up to be the CRX . Gone forever were the 10-inch tires and wheels. Hondas had progressed to a full 13- and 14-inch combination. Wow—now that was progress. Air conditioning and automatic transmissions were offered; sunroofs and AM/FM tape players were options. But all the creature comforts in the world could not replace the true reasons consumers flocked to Honda—the quality of the product—and the Civic was Honda's entry level to this bold new world of Japanese cars.

It didn't take long for a new breed of performance enthusiasts to embrace and modify Honda-made cars. One of the first to achieve success was Oscar Jackson. As early as 1976 Jackson was finding ways to push more horsepower from the CVCC engine. By using the cold-air compression theory, improving exhaust flow and lowering the car's center of gravity, Jackson became a new challenger and champion in SCCA Solo racing. Jackson-prepared Civics were running rings around Porsches, BMWs and English sports cars like the Triumph, TVR and MG.

To the automotive aftermarket, however, the small-car market was still tiny in comparison to small-block Chevys, street rods and trucks. Even though sales success was growing,

popular acceptance as a high-performance, enthusiast's machine was a long way off.

In the late 1970s small trucks, mainly Datsuns, had successfully crossed over to attract an enthusiast niche. From this sprouted compact- or small-truck clubs. In some regions of the country, particularly southern California and Florida, small truck clubs boasted large memberships, a trend that carried over into the 1980s. By 1987, the mini-truck movement was the dominant force in the aftermarket restyling world.

The mini-truck movement was very important to the ongoing development of the Honda Civic as an enthusiast's car. How, you ask? Male owners dominated mini-truck clubs. Male owners wanted female companionship. Young females found the size and shape of compact cars more to their needs and likes than a small truck. Thus mini-truck clubs started allowing customized compact cars to tag along to mini-truck events as "mascot cars." It didn't take long for a large and consistently growing number of compact cars to attend these and other events. Soon show classes were established, and the mini-trucking niche had spun off a new faction and fashion.

In those formative days, three models emerged as the favorites: Ford Escort, Nissan Sentra and Honda Civic. The word was out that tricking out a compact car was not only acceptable but was quickly becoming pre-

Fig. 1-4: Before the days of sport compacting, no self-respecting performance enthusiast would be caught dead buying a four-door. Modern publications, such as *Sport Compact Car* and *Super Street,* regularly feature full-tilt, tricked-out sedans. At the top of the hit list are the Civic EX and DX and the rare VX.

ferred. The biggest stumbling block was the selection of products and services. Thanks to pioneers like Jackson Racing, Eibach Springs and Pacesetter Exhaust, Hondas became the instant frontrunner. Still, the word was not getting out, keeping the sport isolated into focused regions.

In the winter of 1989, the entire scene changed, and with it the elevated popularity of the Honda's Civic as an enthusiast's car. In December 1989, *Sport Compact Car* magazine was spun off from *Mini-Truckin'*, which in the spring of 1988 had spun off from *Truckin'* magazine. Now, for the first time, Civic owners, builders and tuners had a forum in which to display and talk about their cars. The new magazine was perfectly timed to provide both an educational medium and an entertainment outlet for an entirely new generation of hot-rodders.

Within months the Civic had become a cult car for import performance enthusi-asts. Tires, wheels, springs, audio, exhaust and wild paint all were among the first treatments to be performed. Not only were the streets and highways of southern California and Florida sprinkled with tricked-out Hondas, but they were on the move in New York, Maryland, the Carolinas, Georgia, Oregon, Washington, Texas, Nevada, Arizona and Western Canada. Civic mania had begun—and there has been no turning back.

Honda Civics fueled the fires of small-car performance, dragging along with them the CRX and del Sol models. Sales of Honda's Accord and Acura's Integra also greatly benefited from the popularity of the Civic.

One of the newest—and long overdue—ideas from Honda is the Civic Si. Taking the VTEC powerplant technology from the Acura Integra GS-R, this 1999 rocket is the ultimate factory Civic platform. It doesn't come cheap, however. For this reason the

Fig. 1-5: Concept and reality. On the left, this concept rendering from Eibach Springs shows the streetwise appearance of the 1992 Civic. Honda's grocery-getter version on the right is a bit more mundane. However, as you can see, it doesn't take much to transform the hatchback into a real head turner.

Fig. 1-6: In the summer of 1999, Honda launched the Si Coupe. The 1.6L VTEC engine raised the bar of Civic performance to 160 horsepower and a 0-60 time of 7.2 seconds.

basic Civic will still be the foundation on which enthusiasts will rely for entry-level performance.

Thus far all we have talked about is the Civic. But what if you have a CRX instead? Because Honda looked at the world market for the CRX, not necessarily just the American car buyer, it took Honda officials in the United States a number of years to convince the brass of Honda in Japan to import this tiny wonder to American soil.

The CRX was designed as a true entry-level car, one that delivered superior fuel efficiency, would be trouble-free, and, most important for Japanese city dwellers, would be easy to park. If you've ever been to any of Japan's major cities, you know the nightmare of parking. In Tokyo, before you can register a car, you must show proof you have a place to park the vehicle both at home and at work.

The CRX provided a small, nimble car that would deliver 35-40 miles per gallon, seat two comfortably, handle a moderate amount of luggage or cargo, and scoot down the roadway with little effort.

For these reasons, which seemed unique to Japan, it was a risk to expose this car to Americans, who are generally larger in size and demand plenty of leg, head, shoulder and cargo room in their cars. So, when the decision was made to import the CRX, its marketing was targeted to college students and urban commuters. The wildcards were the performance enthusiasts.

Almost instantly the CRX became a go-fast lover's dream. The engine was high-revving, the cornering brisk and easy to calculate, the braking adequate and the reliability superior to any other import or domes-

Fig. 1-7: Even in factory form the CRX looks like a miniature rocket. Check out the factory 13-inch steel wheels, circa 1991.

tic car. And talk about price—these babies were cheap!

For nearly a decade the CRX was a good seller. Sure, the market was still limited, but every CRX that Honda imported Americans bought. When it was announced that the CRX was due for retirement, Honda dealers quickly sold out of the farewell editions. However, the rumor mill was on fire with news of a new Honda sports car, one that would rival the highly successful Mazda Miata.

In 1992 Honda launched the del Sol, a two-seat sports car with a slick targa-style removable roof panel and a retractable rear window. Looking to capitalize on the enormous sales success of the Miata, Honda looked at the del Sol as a better choice—after all, it was a Honda. For Honda, the public reaction was disappointing, to say the least. By this time Miata owners were well organized, and the car had become the biggest selling sports car in history. The del Sol was not viewed as an equal and was not even in the same universe as the Miata as a car that captured the emotions of buyers. The del Sol looked like a warmed-over Fiat X-19 with a wedge-shaped nose and a squared-off tail. The Miata's flowing, retro MG lines and rounded rear were far more pleasing—and it was a true convertible.

It took Honda only 24 months to see the error of its ways and retool a true rival to the Miata. However, it would take until the fall of 1999 to bring that car to market in the form of the S2000 roadster. In the meantime, the frog-like del Sol (which looked especially reptilian in lime green) was phased out of existence.

The model would later re-emerge in the late 1990s as a cult favorite. The reason the del Sol is popular with performance enthusiasts is the fact that it's a Honda, performance items are readily available, the reliability factor remains in place and it offers a low price—mainly due to its original lack of appeal in the market.

So, now that we've gotten Honda's history out of the way, let's talk about the present. First off, how do you determine what to start with—Civic, CRX or del Sol? Here are a few basic questions:

1. Do you want to have seating for more than two people?
   If the answer is yes, move straight to the Civic.

2. Do you want a car that will corner circles around every other car on the road?
   If the answer is yes, move directly to the CRX.

3. Do you want the thrill of open-air driving?
   If the answer is yes, pick the del Sol.

4. Do you want to build it yourself or buy one already built or partially completed?
   If you want to build it yourself, keep reading this book to discover all your options. If you want one done, keep reading to see if the one you want is done right. If you want one partially completed, stop reading and check into the nearest psycho ward.

To help you make a better decision, here are the pros and cons of each model.

Civic

Pros:
- Space for four.
- Good handling.
- Massive selection of years and models to choose from.
- Every performance item known to man is available.
- Factory replacement parts are easy to find.
- Not a bad-looking model in the bunch.

Cons:
- Low horsepower engines.

- Too many automatics were produced.
- Seating for four means you'll be driving your little brother and his friends to soccer practice.
- Everyone's got one.

CRX

Pros:

- Can be made to handle like nobody's business.
- Shares drivetrain parts with Civics of same years.
- Cool styling.
- Race-car-like feel.
- Only a few people have one.

Cons:

- Tiny interior.
- Replacement body parts are hard to find.
- Can't be seen in the side view mirror of semi trucks.
- Cheap interior with too much molded plastic.
- Only a few people have one.

del Sol

Pros:

- Removable roof panel.
- Performance and styling parts available.
- True sports car handling.
- When done right, a real chick magnet.
- Cool interior with proper gauges.

Cons:

- Low safety rating.
- No room for luggage, audio equipment or tools.
- Goofy factory colors.
- Funky styling with too much wheel well gap.
- Replacement body parts impossible to find.
- Expensive to insure.

That was easy. Now that you've selected the Honda you want (Civic, CRX or del Sol), here are some basic rules for selecting the right car.

Where to Find It

There are many places to locate the right car. If you're buying new, your local dealership is a good place to start, provided you selected a Civic. Don't be intimidated by the salesperson. It's his or her job to show you the car. However, whatever you do, don't talk to the salesperson or anyone else at a dealership about modifying the car. This could lead to questions about warranty and finance restrictions. And whatever you do, don't fall in love with the low monthly payment of a lease. Leases are set up to the advantage of the bank. Plus, modifying your car on a lease may come around to a bite in the rear—of the lease. If you turn in a leased car full of modifications, you may be charged the cost of turning the car back to factory condition.

Before making a new Civic purchase, check Internet sites, such as Edmunds (www.edmunds.com), for vehicle information, true dealer invoice factors and fleet-buying alternatives. If you want to include some modifications, like performance suspension springs and aftermarket tires and wheels, dealers may be able to include these items in the purchase price and build them into the monthly payment. Some dealers, such as Tipton Honda in El Cajon, California, offer an entire tuner shop for after-purchase decisions.

For used (or previously owned) Hondas, check your local Trader publications, newspapers or used car lots. A car club can be another excellent source for finding the right unit.

The Civic Evolution

YEAR	ENGINE	HORSEPOWER	0-60	WEIGHT	PRICE
1973	1168cc	52	14.4	1,540	$2,376
1974	1237cc	52	14.2	1,576	$2,495
1975	1488cc	53	15.6	1,704	$2,999
1977	1488cc	60	14.0	1,750	$3,499
1979	1488cc	60	13.6	1,750	$3,999
1980	1488cc	67	11.2	1,822	$4,599
1984	1488cc	76	10.2	1,910	$7,125
1986	1.5L	92	9.4	1,989	$7,499
1988	1.6L	108	9.1	1,993	$7,990
1992	1.6L	125	8.5	2,340	$11,999
1996	1.6L	127	8.9	2,465	$15,999
1999	1.6L	160	7.2	2,612	$18,299

What to Look For

If you're looking at a car from a private owner, bring along a common refrigerator magnet, a bucket with car-wash products, sponge and drying cloths, a plastic-coated card and a pencil with an eraser.

When you get serious about the car, first drive it with the windows down and the audio system off. Listen for squeaks and rattles. Roll up the windows and check for wind and suspension noise. Make sure the windows seal tight. If there are gaps, it could mean the car has been hit and repaired.

While moving at a fair rate of speed (best done in an open parking lot) firmly press the brakes. The car should stop straight and consistent. Next, slowly accelerate with your hands barely touching the steering wheel. Once again, the car should operate straight and consistent.

If it shifts, brakes and runs well, do a complete physical inspection. Using the magnet, check all the body panels. If the car has plastic body filler, the magnet won't stick to it—evidence of repair. Use the plastic-coated card to measure the gap in the doors, hood and other body seams. The pencil can be laid in the grooves of the hood and trunk to measure consistency. The eraser is used to tap body panels and check the sound for rust and filler.

Pop open all the doors, hood and trunk: check the seals for cracks and splits. Look for overspray, a sure sign of damage repair. Look at the undercarriage, the place overspray is usually found. Pull the engine dipstick. If the oil is clean and thin, it usually means it's in good order or has just had an oil change. If the oil is dirty and thin, the car may not have been well cared for (therefore low miles mean nothing). If the oil is clean and thick, this could mean the seller loaded it up with heavier weight oil to cover up valve train noise. If the oil is thick and dirty, run away.

If your prospective car has passed these tests, ask the seller if you can wash the car. It may sound strange, but when you wash and dry the car, you'll find every imperfection on it. Every ding, dent and scratch will jump out at you, even if the car is painted white.

Check the tires for even wear. If the tires are not in great shape, who cares?—they are going to be the first things to be replaced. However, if the tires are new and the car is advertised as having less than 30,000 miles on it, that's a question mark in my mind. The tires that come on Hondas from the factory should be good for 40,000-50,000 miles. If the car has 24,000 miles and new tires, what's the story?

Finally, open the trunk and pull the mat up—check for a rusted floorboard.

If everything checks out, haggle over the price, get the ride and let's move this show to Chapter 2.

The Basics of
Personalizing

Fig. 2-1: Civic and CRX models are popular for import drag racing because of the vehicle's light weight and near 50/50 balance. Building a car for this purpose demands compromising some street-handling capabilities.

There it is—your new (or new to you) Civic. Running through your mind are all these wild concepts and ideas about how fast it's going to go or how slick your ride will be as you cruise the boulevard some future Saturday night. But for now it sits on pizza-cutter tires and steel wheels. Under the hood is the stock air box, cam cover, exhaust manifold and other various uglies all covered with three years of dirt and grease. The suspension features about five inches of wheel well gap. The interior resembles four felt squares on soiled carpeting, and the fine AM/FM cassette tape player has a missing load door. Needless to say, as is, this car is not going to get you any dates.

But hope springs eternal. You have a vision. Flawless paint, 18-inch wheels, precision suspension, tuned exhaust, leather interior, pounding audio system, 0-60 in 5.9 seconds. Now we're talking about a chick magnet. But how do you get there?

Although there are many ways to outfit your Civic—street, strip, sport or show—there are only two ways in which to achieve the final result. The two methods are called addition and subtraction. Both will get the job done. Both will result in a good looking, well running version. Both will take time. Both will cost you money. However, one will cost you more time and money than the other will. Before we get to all that, however, let's determine what you want to do with your import performance machine.

Like most of us, you will want this car to be your primary mode of daily transportation—to use to and from work, school, family functions, club activities, events, etc. If this is the case, it is important that

There is no wrong way to build a trick Civic. However, there is a better way. Street, Strip, Sport or Show, you can't have it all. Or maybe, if you're ingenious, you can have a little of each.

the car has the ability to perform commonly needed functions with relative ease. For example:

- The ability to carry one or more passengers.
- Room for a modest amount of luggage, tools or cargo.
- Space for a spare tire and first aid kit (never underestimate the importance of these items).
- The ability to be driven in foul as well as fair weather.
- Reliable, worry free operation.

From this point we can explore the different avenues for contemporary Civic modifications and personalization. Here are the five basic modification categories:

1. Strip

A Civic designed for import drag racing.

Pros:

- Superior acceleration.
- Fastest growing participation motorsport niche.
- Expensive alloy wheels not needed.
- No big expense on cosmetic enhancements (chrome, custom paint, etc.).
- Fun and cheap for taking part in events.

Cons:

- Poor cornering (point-and-shoot suspension technology).
- Car is gutted of creature comforts to reduce weight.
- Major dollars are needed to achieve greater horsepower (pistons, rods, studs, etc.).
- More safety equipment is needed (scatter shield, helmet etc.).
- Car looks ugly Monday through Friday.

2. Sport

A Civic built for competitive motorsports.

Pros:

- Better engine response.
- Superior handling.
- Turning left and right allows you to get to know the limits of your car.
- Fun and cheap for taking part in events.
- No big expense on cosmetic enhancements (chrome, custom paint, etc.)

Cons:

- Stiffer suspension makes for less comfortable street driving.
- Special tire and wheel size is needed for optimum results (13 or 14 inch).
- The more modifications you do the tougher the class you're in.

Figs. 2-2 & 2-3: Here are two versions of the same car. The black Civic hatchback is a purpose-built SCCA-style solo racer. The white hatchback shows off the classic California look—low, sleek and clean.

Fig. 2-4: When it comes to building a show Civic, break out the imagination and the checkbook. Preparing a truly effective show car takes vision and precise planning and flawless execution. And you can't stop at just designing the car; presentation is nearly as important. This means you'll need to set aside funds for a display.

Fig. 2-5: Owning a full-on show Civic will require three things: lots of cash, lots of clean soft cloths and lots of space for trophies. This hatchback, built for *Lowrider Magazine*, is perhaps the finest show Civic in the country.

- Not enough events.
- For events other than solo racing, major safety equipment is required (roll cage, driving suit, helmet, etc.).

3. Show

A Civic made to elevate your ego.

Pros:

- Everyone will be looking at your car.
- Pride of ownership.
- Envy of everyone on the cruise scene.
- Fills up your house with trophies.
- Will be magazine material.

Cons:

- You'll likely need a trailer and tow vehicle to get it to shows.

- You'll be less willing to drive the car (making it a garage and trailer queen).
- Major expense on custom paint, chrome, and all excessive stuff.
- Car will be hard to sell.
- You'll never get your money back.
- Fills up your house with trophies.

4. Lowrider

Made to hop, skip and jump.

Pros:

- Can leap tall speed bumps in a single bound.
- Impressive to others at stoplights (make that bad-boy hop).
- Uniqueness always draws a crowd.

Fig. 2-6: For extreme visual effect, no category of Civic can match a lowrider. Over-the-edge paint, gold plating, no-holds barred interiors and suspensions featuring precision-engineered hydraulics are all major components to building a unbelievable street cruiser.

Cons:

- Hydraulic suspensions are rough riding and poor handling.
- No space in the trunk due to all the pumps and batteries.
- Major expense on custom paint, chrome, and interior.
- Excessive hopping and jumping can bend expensive wire wheels and break shocks and springs.
- If not professional built, you can watch and hear the frame and body twist and stress.
- Car will be hard to sell.
- CD player takes a beating.

Fig. 2-7: Purpose-built racecars, such as this 1996 Civic, can be made functional for the street. This version features an adjustable coilover suspension system to vary ride height and quality. In the most extreme setting (three inches lower than stock) it looks great on the street. In the optimum handling setting, the car can run rings around European sports cars that carry three times the price.

Fig. 2-8: Recently the street trend has been to mirror the look of cars of Touring Car series. This car shows how effective use of vinyl graphics combined with trick styling packaged with sponsor logos and bolt-on accessories can turn even the most mundane Civic into a street screamer.

5. Street

A Civic designed for multi-purpose living.

Pros:

- Good handling.
- Choice of build options.
- Creature comforts can remain.
- Can be used at almost any type of import car event.
- Can be used everyday.
- Excellent street appeal.
- Easier to sell when you're ready.

Cons:

- Doesn't do one thing exceptionally well.
- You'll always need to keep it clean.
- Expensive alloy wheels and high performance tires a must.
- Will likely cause you to hear the following question from boy/girlfriend: "What's more important, me or your car?"

With the possible exception of the last "con," the street version is by far the most practical and enjoyable version of Civic to build. In a well-executed street Civic you can have a little of everything: strip, sport, show and even lowrider.

Now comes the part about the two methods in which to build your Civic: Addition or Subtraction.

Addition, the practice of adding parts and features as you go, is, contrary to common logic, the most common method used to construct a Civic. It is also the biggest mistake you can make. This method often results in a greater number of installed and later discarded accessories and parts, which can quickly drain a bank account. All the while each unplanned action only serves as a quick fix for your modification habit. Another word commonly used for this type of customizing is called "impulse" buying. You'll eventually have something close to what you originally wanted, provided you have enough time and money.

Subtraction is knowing what you want your Honda to end up like and working in reverse to get there. This might seem backwards, but it is a very sound method to realizing the final achievement.

Working in subtraction requires you to develop a customized "build-sheet." For example, start by visualizing the Civic you really want to drive. Next, take a look at the Civic you actually have. Now begin to assemble on paper the components it will take to get to your dream version.

For this exercise, lets build a trick street version of a two-year-old Civic using both addition and subtraction methods. The car is in complete factory trim. The body has only parking lot dings, and the paint is in good condition.

Building through Addition

Step One. You want a lower, performance-looking stance. You purchase and install three-inch lowering springs.

Step Two. Now the 14-inch tires and wheels look "tucked" into the fender wells, which is good, but no amount of lowering will change the fact that these are stock tires and wheels. You purchase 17x7 inch wheels and 215/40-17 tires.

Step Three. Performance becomes an issue because now your car is slower than when it was stock. The reason? The greater drag co-efficacy caused by the tires' larger tread surface. You buy into the performance exhaust theory thinking you'll regain the lost engine response. It sounds like a performance car. You buy a three-inch exhaust system and throw on a chrome tip the size of a manhole cover. Is the problem solved?

Step Four. Now that you're obsessed with horsepower, you need an air-intake system, but you're a little short on funds after the expensive $450 super-mondo exhaust system. You

buy price and within a few days a short-pipe system arrives at your doorstep. You install the trendy painted piece and prepare for neck-snapping acceleration gains. Reality checks in when you gain about three to five ponies.

Step Five. With major funds depleted, you feed your habit by doing smaller, less expensive additions: line wrap, small polished or chrome platted trinkets, pedal covers, etc.

Step Six. You discover the ride quality of the suspension combination is too harsh. The problem is the lubricant leaking from your shocks. They have blown out because the spring rate was too light for the ride height reduction. Besides, the car handles poor because it is too low. After wising up, you buy new performance springs and struts/shocks. You sell the first set of springs to some other schmuck building his car using the Addition method.

Step Seven. You smarten up and start doing things in the Subtraction mode.

Building through Subtraction

Step One. If the car is street-worthy, use it for a few weeks as a general means of transportation. This might seem like torture, but it is one of the best ways to get to know the full condition of your car. If you're starting with a new Civic, these few weeks will help you better understand what Honda had in mind when they engineered the car. It will also give you a better feel for the horsepower and handling gains you'll realize later.

Step Two. Create the special "build sheet" for your car. This will start out as a wish list. Over time it will become a blueprint. For a typical street version, you may find it helpful to know your local and state laws that govern emissions-control devices, body modifications, lighting, exhaust noise, etc. This will head off potential problems later.

Engine

PRODUCT	STRIP	SPORT	SHOW	LOWRIDER	STREET
Cam Gear	•	•			•
Cold Air System	•	•	•		•
Performance Pulleys	•	•	•		•
Chrome Covers			•	•	•
Performance Ignition	•	•			•
Turbocharger	•				•
Nitrous Oxide	•		•		
Performance Pistons	•	•			
Extrude Hone	•	•			•
Header	•	•	•		
Exhaust	•	•			•
Performance Cam	•	•			

Suspension

PRODUCT	STRIP	SPORT	SHOW	LOWRIDER	STREET
Performance Springs	•	•			•
Lowering Springs			•	•	•
Hopping Springs				•	
Performance Shocks	•	•			•
Anti-Roll Bars		•			•
Upper Strut Bar		•	•		•
13" Wheels		•		•	
14" Wheels	•	•			
15" Wheels	•				
16" Wheels			•		•
17" Wheels			•	•	•
18" Wheels			•	•	•
20" Wheels			•	•	
Performance Tires	•	•	•	•	•
Urethane Bushings	•	•	•		
Hydraulics				•	

Step Three. Determine the car's most critical area of need. If you want massive horsepower gains, this is the time to perform extensive engine modifications. If only minor engine modifications and dress-up are likely, you will want to consider the body and paint work first. If the ride height is unbearable and the tires are on their last tread of steel, start with the tires, wheels and springs.

Step Four. Learn discipline. Remember, unless you're a lottery winner, you can't do everything at once—and you really don't want to anyway. It's more fun to stretch out the process. This allows you to get to know the tricks and trends along the way.

Step Five. Research the equipment in each area of the car: engine, exterior, suspension, interior, transmission, audio, paint and body. The more you know about the history and reliability of the products you want, the better shopper you'll be.

Step Six. Prioritize your building—and begin.
Here are the most common "bolt-on" aftermarket products and how they fit into each of the basic Civic build groups.

Brakes

PRODUCT	STRIP	SPORT	SHOW	LOWRIDER	STREET
Performance Pads	•	•			•
Slotted Rotors		•	•		•
Performance Calipers		•	•		•
Steel Brake Lines	•	•	•		•
Drag Shoot	•		•		

Transmission

PRODUCT	STRIP	SPORT	SHOW	LOWRIDER	STREET
Performance Clutch	•	•			•
Performance Plate	•	•			
Short Linkage	•	•	•		•
Scatter Shield	•	•			

Exterior Styling

PRODUCT	STRIP	SPORT	SHOW	LOWRIDER	STREET
Front Air Dam	•	•	•	•	•
Side Skirts			•	•	•
Rear Valance			•	•	•
Rear Spoiler		•	•	•	•
Oversize Wing	•		•		•
Fiberglass Hood	•	•	•		
Driving Lamps			•	•	•
Light Covers			•		
Tinted Windows			•	•	•
Custom Paint			•	•	•
Sponsor Decals	•	•			•

Interior Components

PRODUCT	STRIP	SPORT	SHOW	LOWRIDER	STREET
Leather			•	•	•
Racing Seats	•	•			•
Harness Belts	•	•	•		
Gauges	•	•	•		•
Roll Cage	•	•			
Roll Bar			•		•
Custom Steering Wheel	•	•	•		
Sunroof			•	•	•
Pedal Covers			•	•	•
Custom Shift Knob	•	•	•	•	•
No Rear Seat	•	•			

Knowing what type of Civic you want to end up with will greatly reduce wasted time, effort and money. The second major benefit to using a set plan is that the end result will likely be a car you'll be happy with for years, rather than months.

How the Experts Do It

Most experienced import performance car builders agree that successful construction begins with the tires, wheels and springs. (Picking the right suspension components will be covered in the next chapter.) Let's first select the tire and wheel combination that best fits your needs and wants.

Large-diameter 18-inch wheels provide a killer look, but the rubberband sidewalls of 35- and 40-aspect tires make for a rough ride. That's right, the *tires* make for a rough ride. Most drivers falsely believe it's the shortened springs that cause that kidney-jolting, loose-filling-in-the-tooth ride. Actually, the tires play as big a role in determining ride quality as the springs.

When you know the language of tires you start to get a better idea of the different levels and qualities associated with performance tires—for example, that of a "205/45-17 tire." What do the numbers mean? 205: The tread width in relation to the aspect ratio. 45: The aspect ratio or sidewall height. 17: The wheel measurement required.

So your friend buys a new set of tires and wheels for his Accord and offers to sell you the 225/40-17 set he removed (he is likely building his car in the addition method). Should you consider the purchase? NO!

First, the tire is too wide to accommodate any ride height reduction (lowering). Second, the back spacing of the wheels is likely to be wrong, causing the wheels to rub against the inner lip of the fenders. Third, with the current war between wheel compa-

nies, it is highly likely you can get the set you really want at a competitive price.

If you're building your Civic for everyday street use, the largest tire and wheel combination needed is 17x7-inch wheels on 215/40-17 tires. This will provide an excellent appearance and allow for reasonable road compliance. However, as mentioned before, 17-inch or greater tires and wheels will steal acceleration. For this reason many street performance enthusiasts compromise overall appearance for quicker acceleration by using 16-inch wheels.

This brings us to another key point: weight. Before purchasing any wheel, pick it up and compare the weight of one wheel to another. The heavier the wheel, the more energy it will require to move it. Multiply that number by four and you will find significant power losses are realized by big wheels. This is not to say all 17-inch wheels are created equal in weight. Aluminum is lighter than steel, component wheels are lighter than cast wheels, billet wheels are ideal as boat anchors, and magnesium wheels are lighter than air. (Magnesium wheels were first used in racing because of their extremely light weight. The styles became popular; thus the term "mag wheel" was born. While these wheels are light, the durability factor does not fare well on the street in everyday use.)

For the weekend racer or sport driver, ultra-lightweight 14-inch wheels and low and fat performance tires spell faster times and superior cornering. For parking lot racers (SCCA-style Solo racing), an extra set of shorter diameter tires and wheels pay off in quicker laps. The downside is that they look funky for everyday use, the softer compound rubber wears quickly on the street and they are extremely dangerous on wet surfaces. If you're going to go cone racing, you will want to budget for two sets of tires and wheels— one set for street and one set for sport. The same holds true if you're going to be a week-

Sample Build Sheet

YEAR _____   MODEL _____   TRIM _____

ITEM #	ITEM	BRAND	PRICE
1	Springs	Eibach Sportline	($220)
2	Sway Bars	Eibach Pro Control	($125)
3	Shocks/Struts	Koni	($175)
4	Strut Bar	DC Sport(polished)	($150)
5	Tires	205/40-17 Yokohama or Toyo	($600)
6	Wheels	JM Motorsports Stage 5 (17x7)	($500)
7	Bushings	O.E.	
8	Exhaust	Jackson Racing	($500)
9	Intake	AEM SportComp (clear silver)	($225)
10	Cam	O.E.	
11	Cam Timing	AEM Tru-Time Cam Timing Gear	($150)
12	Accessories	AEM Tru-Power Pulleys	($125)
13	Ignition Coil	Nology ProFire and Honda Cap	($125)
14	Ignition Wires	Vitek	($90)
15	Plugs	Silverstone	($40)
16	Header	None	
17	Nitrous Oxide	None	
18	Computer Chip	None	
19	Front Air Dam	Wings West or Xenon	($275)
20	Side Skirts	Wings West or Xenon	($250)
21	Rear Valance	Wings West or Xenon	($240)
22	Rear Deck Wing	Wings West or Xenon	($300)
23	Paint	Rob Taylor	($350)
24	Window Tint	Tint Man	($100)
25	Paint Scheme	Modern Image—vinyl graphics	($450)
26	Exhaust Tip(s)	Cone or Shotgun	($75)
27	Race Tach	AutoMeter	($75)
28	CD Player	Sony	($400)
29	Amps	Pioneer	($250)
30	Speakers	MTX	($400)
31	Installation	Custom Audio Sounds	($450)
32	Seats	O.E.	
33	Interior Trim	Leather	($1,100)
34	Pedal Covers	Toucan	($80)
35	Shift Knob	Momo	($80)
36	Roll Bar/Cage	Three Point	($250)
37	Steering Wheel	O.E.	
38	Linkage	Neuspeed	($150)
39	Clutch	Exedy or Clutch Master	($375)
40	Brake Upgrade	AEM two-piston kit	($500)

TOTAL FOR UPGRADES   **$9,660**

end drag racer—you'll need a set for the street and a set for the track.

Just a few years ago, a drag slick for import racing was nonexistent. Most serious racers were forced to adapt tires made for domestic drag racing or shave the tread for performance tires. Today, oddly enough, famous drag racing tire manufacturers, such as M&H, Mickey Thompson and Firestone, now offer drag slicks for front wheel drive cars. These tires are designed to get hot and sticky for a more potent launch.

Carefully research the marketplace and be a smart shopper. With the resources of retail, Internet and mail order, you should be able to find the tire and wheel combination to correctly fit your car.

The Build Sheet

Perhaps the best way to prioritize your budget constrictions is to create a customized build sheet, which will list all the components that you envision will make the ideal Civic. Again, using magazine mail order ads, Internet sites and local retail stores, attach a price to each of the items you have on the sheet. With all the prices thus listed, you can begin to make intelligent decisions on how best to achieve your goal. If you have unlimited funds, you can build by category:

engine, suspension, interior, exterior, etc. However, I have yet to meet the Civic owner with unlimited funds. Therefore, it will be necessary to budget your build up. Your customized build sheet will offer you a unique reference point to work from.

Using this sample build sheet and a monthly budget of $500 per month to devote to the project, how would you build a 1997 Civic EX Coupe?

Getting Ready to Move On

By now you've got to be ready to move on. However, before moving on to Chapter 3 here is one last reminder: always remember to build your Civic with a degree of patience. It is important to set your performance and appearance goals and stick to them. Each time you sway from the straight and narrow you delay or sidetrack the completion of your goal. I'm not saying you can't amend your plan; just do so in a logical manner—one that enhances the final product.

If you start out wanting a Civic for drag racing and switch in midstream to a show version, the costs will quickly escalate—often out of control. This is why it is crucial to fully think through the type of car you want to own and image you want to project.

Suspension 101: Get Down And Get Around

Fig. 3-1: Here are the main upgrades to your suspension—springs, shock/struts and bars. Selecting the right combination can make your Civic handle like it's on rails. Quality is the key ingredient when purchasing suspension products. You get what you pay for.

CHapTer 3

It has been said that the tires and wheels make the car. It has also been discovered that the right springs make the tires and wheels. It is also true that lower is not better. While these three components are important, setting up your Civic with the proper suspension goes way beyond determining the right tires, wheels and springs for the type of driving or motorsports you plan on doing. In fact, the most critical part of any true performance car is the inner workings of the suspension.

There is a complex theory to proper suspension geometry. Keeping it in simple terms, suspension is about controlling the handling of your car by properly harnessing the effects of the kinetic energy generated and heat displacement created during operation. To fully understand the use and reuse of suspension energy, you must first understand the purpose of your Civic's suspension. The main function of the suspension is to allow the movement of the tires and wheels to be independent of the chassis—thus absorbing and transferring energy for the benefit of the car's relationship with the road. Doing this properly will maintain a comfortable ride for the passengers and vehicle control for the driver. To effectively achieve this requires the use of several components: springs, shocks, bushings, anti-roll bars, upper strut bars and tires.

The most effective suspension helps maintain road adhesion—in other words, the suspension assists the driver to achieve optimum control even during extreme and demanding conditions. Maximizing your car's suspension takes the right combination of components for the types of driving you intend to do. A well-engineered and -executed Civic suspension setup will result in improved vehicle stability, quicker point-zero

Getting to know your Civic from the ground up. Springs, shocks, anti-sway bars, bushings, tires, wheels and how they all work together.

Fig. 3-2: This is our project Civic before the first of many modifications. Note the nosebleed stance and grandma-style factory wheels.

rebound, better tire adhesion and a more nimble response factor.

As mentioned in Chapter 2, the method most often advised for modifying your Civic's factory suspension is using the "subtraction" approach. Introducing performance aftermarket suspension components with your Civic's factory platform requires more research than just buying a set of springs. However, because springs are the most common suspension purchase, this is a good starting point.

Springs

Suspension springs represent two areas of vital importance to Civic owners. First, their handling is superior to O.E. equipment. Second, they make the car look better by reducing its ride height and eliminating wheel well gap (the space between the top of the tire and the inside apex of the wheel well opening). The first and sometimes fatal mistake Civic owners make is lowering the car with the wrong springs—or worse yet, cutting the factory springs. It is important to remember just because a car looks like a race car doesn't mean it will handle like a race car.

Springs are what are called "load sensitive" mechanisms. All Civics are equipped with coil springs, both front and rear. Coil springs come in a variety of rates and heights; however, there are two basic spring rate configurations: linear and progressive. Linear

springs maintain a constant rate throughout each winding. Progressive-rate springs are engineered to deliver at varying rates in the upper and lower windings, with improved damping during compression and rebound. The first CVCC produced and all Civic, CRX and del Sol suspensions to follow were

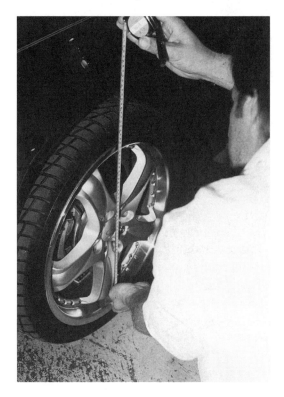

Fig. 3-3: The installation of the Sportline springs began by first replacing the factory steel and rubber with JM Motorsport Stage 5 wheels and 205/40-17 Falken performance tires. To get an idea of the ride height reduction with the factory springs in place, measure the distance from the bottom of the wheel and the lower apex of the fender well opening.

Fig. 3-4: Coil springs have different levels of rate and ride-height reduction. To match the right springs with your project, first settle on the type of driving and motorsport activity you will most likely be participating in. Also pay close attention to the grade of material used to produce the spring. This is critical to the lasting performance of the component.

mance springs are designed to help the car realize its best handling capabilities. Lowering springs are made to offer a more drastic reduction in ride height regardless of what they do to the car's suspension performance."

Here is the first key point in suspension alteration. You must ask yourself if you want your car to perform or to look like it performs. Nearly all aftermarket springs for Civics will improve the appearance of your car. Not all will optimize its handling.

The ideal ride-height reduction using coil springs on struts for any year Civic is .75 to 1.75 inches. This allows for the existing suspension components to continue to work

designed with Honda factory coil springs, which are linear in design. These springs provide a smooth, comfortable ride but are designed for ease of factory assembly and the most cost-effective production process possible.

Honda engineers and designers are limited by two very important factors—time and space—the time it takes to install any component on the assembly line and the space in which the component must fit and perform. While the original shocks, springs, bushings, sway bars and tires provide the masses with an acceptable ride and adequate performance, enthusiasts feel something more can be achieved.

Manufacturers of performance springs are governed only by space. Because they are limited to the area that the Honda designers have made available, performance springs offer stiffer rates and reduced length. Both of these factors play a highly important role in the handling of your Civic.

Now, before we go any further, you should be aware that there are two marketing categories of springs you will encounter, performance springs and lowering springs. According to Gary Peek, vice president of sales and marketing for Eibach Springs, "perfor-

Fig. 3-5: If you're going to attempt to install aftermarket springs, start by installing an above-ground lift. On second thought, scratch that step, as this will cost you more than a new Civic. If you have access to a lift you can complete the job in a few hours. If you're working on a flat surface, make sure it's a solid concrete slab. Use plenty of safety precautions like jack stands, wheel chalk blocks, eye protection, hair net, etc. Start by unbolting the spring strut assembly from the lower control arms.

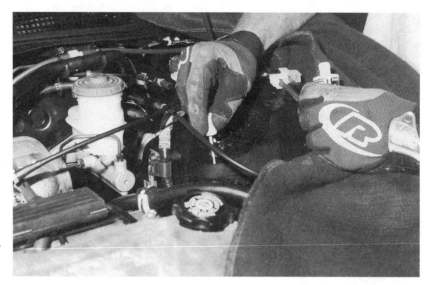

Fig. 3-6: With the lower portion free, remove the upper strut fasteners. Before pulling the spring/strut assembly from the car, mark the strut clocking position on the strut tower. A little White-Out does the job nicely.

in relative harmony with new performance springs. All too often import performance enthusiasts fall into the trap of lowering a car beyond safe levels. While this may offer a track-like look, it results in a major problem. When the car is sitting too low, there is no suspension left for spring and shock travel. When the car encounters a bump or change in road levels, even the smallest in nature, a

Fig. 3-7: After the spring/strut assembly is free from the suspension, use a spring compressor to safely relieve the pre-load energy from the compressed factory spring. As you can see, the Sportline spring (left) is considerably shorter than the factory spring.

bottoming out effect takes place. The only device stopping or absorbing the kinetic energy generated by the bump is the bump stop. This is the second-to-last thing you want to have happen because a bump stop is not made to be a compression component. The bump in the road moves the entire car. There is no shock-damping and no spring travel remaining to buffer the energy force or respond to the reaction of gravity waiting to pull the car back to the pavement. With the tires, wheels and chassis all deeply affected by this action, loss of tire contact with the road is going to happen. All this action occurs in a split second. Multiply this over the thousands of bumps and road surface changes you encounter each day and you begin to understand the high rate of fatigue you are causing—all in the name of appearance.

By installing performance springs with ride-height reductions of .75 to 1.75 inches, you will discover that everyday driving is far more enjoyable, but you can still retain factory-like comfort. When you use these ride-height reductions, road compliance (or ride harshness) is more affected by the tires than the springs. Performance springs deliver better handling and elevate driver confidence. Highway on-ramps become more fun, twisting roads are turned into playgrounds and driving in inclement weather is less stressful.

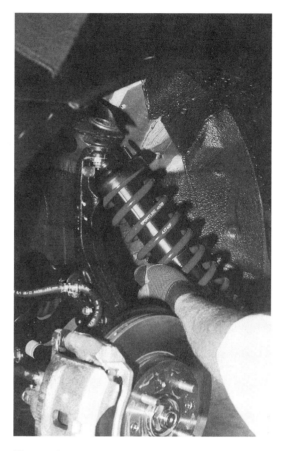

Fig. 3-8: Reassemble the strut and spring assembly and install.

Fig. 3-9: Tighten all fasteners. This is where that clocking trick comes into play.

Although a .75 to 1.75 inches reduction is preferred, that's not to say you can't lower your Civic beyond these points. You can lower the car as much as three inches using coil-over springs and struts. However, be aware that lowering your car this much will result in severe alignment problems. The .75 to 1.75 inches of lowering window keeps the car within factory alignment tolerances. The lower the car gets the greater the alignment problem. If you're planning to lower your Civic below the recommended levels, an aftermarket alignment kit will be necessary. These kits usually consist of recalculated front a-arms and longer rear trailing arms. Without the use of an aftermarket alignment package, you can expect premature tire wear, especially on the inside portion of the tread face.

It is also a preferred practice never to heat-set or cut coil springs. Performing either one of these techniques will result in unknown spring rate changes and may cause the springs to snap under the increased fatigue. Improper lowering also can twist and bend struts and shock rods, rendering them totally ineffective.

If appearance is important, and it should be, the simple rule of AR/OP=AWWG (aspect ratio to open space equals acceptable wheel well gap) always applies. To determine this equation, measure your tire's sidewall. Next, measure the open space or gap between the top of the sidewall and the apex of the fender well opening. You should always have the same or a lesser amount of wheel well gap than the tire's sidewall measurement. For example, a 205/45-17-inch tire has a sidewall measurement of 1.50 inches. The corrected wheel well gap should be less than 1.50 inches.

Fig. 3-10: To determine what is enough lowering for the look of performance, a simple rule has been put into play. The distance between the top of the tire and the lower apex of the fender well should be equal or less than the sidewall aspect of the tire.

Fig. 3-11: With all four corners completed, measure the wheel-to-fender well distance. Wow—a full two-inch reduction in ride height.

Correctly designed and manufactured performance springs combine the best of both worlds—function and fashion. However, two old sayings hold tremendous truth when it comes to springs: 1) not all springs are created equal; and 2) you get what you pay for.

Remember the line, "just because it looks like a race car doesn't mean it will handle like a race car"? This should be your motto when shopping for aftermarket springs. Lowering springs cost less than performance springs. The number-one reason is simple to understand—it takes a lot less research and development to make lowering springs.

Consumer research plays a major role in determining the brand and style of springs to install on your Civic. Prioritize your needs and desires, then research the springs that best fit those priorities. For example, if handling performance is number one on your list, look for springs made by those companies that supply race teams, such as Eibach, Hyperco and H&R. If appearance is the optimum goal, Suspension Techniques, Sprint or Intrax are worth considering. For street performance, Eibach, H&R, Neuspeed, Jackson Racing and Tokico all have good offerings.

All aftermarket springs are going to perform the most important handling function—lowering the car's center of gravity. But the materials used to produce the springs and the amount of research and dedication to proper development and manufacturing are the keys to spring selection.

Shocks

After replacing the factory-issued springs with performance counterparts, the next big improvement is shocks. The importance of aftermarket shocks (called dampers in Europe) should never be overlooked. For the overall handling capabilities of your Civic, performance shocks are as vital as performance springs.

While coil springs are the basis for suspension movement and performance, without shocks the bouncing action would never stop. The reason shocks/struts/dampers exist is to control the unwanted movement of the springs. It is the job of the shock absorbers, not the springs, to maintain the contact between the tires and the road.

Here's how road compliance works. When your car encounters a bump in the road, the tire is first in line to deflect and absorb the energy created by the bump. What energy the tire sidewall does not deflect becomes movement up into the chassis. The next line of defense is the spring. The force of the raising movement combines with the mass of the tire, wheel and brake to cause kinetic energy that forces the spring to compress. The spring stores this force and converts it to potential energy in route to full and complete reversal, or rebound. The energy is now ready to return to the tire, where the energy pushes the tire back to the pavement, bringing with it the tremendous inertia created by the weight of the vehicle. This will continue until all the energy is displaced. The items that keep this from continuing are the shock absorbers.

Shocks work to maintain tire patch contact with the pavement. To do this, the vertical motion of the car must be halted as soon as possible. As mentioned earlier in the chapter, a spring is a load-sensitive device. Shocks, on the other hand, are speed-sensitive. The force of the two end points is dictated by the speed of the movement that is

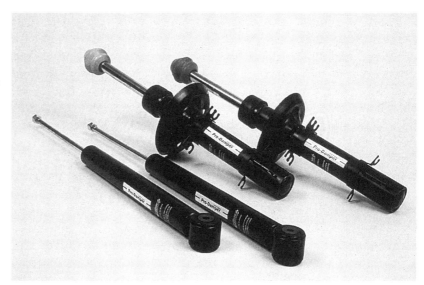

Fig. 3-12: Whether you call them shocks, struts or dampers, these items are vital to the safe and predictable performance of your Civic's handling. As with the springs, quality plays an important factor. Performance shocks are necessary when lower, performance springs are installed. Factory shocks are not valved to handle the reduced travel caused by lower springs.

applying the force, which is measured in the distance and speed traveled between the two end points. When a bump is encountered, the vertical motion meets resistance by two forces, the spring and the shock. When the wheel is rapidly projected up or down, the shock handles the resistances with a dominant force of its own. At this point our old friend kinetic energy meets with a new factor. No longer is the spring needed to store all the energy caused by the bump. The shock enforces a "work" factor to displace the energy (work equals force times distance ($w = f \times d$)). What occurs is that the wheel and tire do not need to compress the spring as far. The rebound distance and time are drastically reduced. The overall result is a tire that quickly returns to the pavement or doesn't lose contact at all.

Springs that reduce ride height, whether they are performance or lowering springs, shorten the distance the suspension travels. This reduced distance is reflected in shock travel as well. Shock absorbers are designed to control the aforementioned energy levels. They are engineered to control bounce by valve rate. When ride-height adjustments are made, the shock absorber can be greatly affected. If the shock is compressed too far, even small bumps cause the shock's rod to force unreasonable pressure on the internal valve rate. This will result in rupturing the seals and will destroy any handling and ride-quality value of the shock.

Original-equipment shock absorbers are not designed to accommodate performance and/or lowering springs. Factory specification shocks do not have enough valve capacity to control the advanced forces caused by stiffer, shorter springs. Some shocks are so under-valved that many aftermarket spring companies will not provide warranties for their products unless approved performance shocks are used.

The answer is to replace the factory shocks/struts with performance aftermarket items. Shocks and struts feature compatible valve ratings that are engineered to work in conjunction with lower springs. Therefore, these shocks allow you to take full advantage of the performance springs and tires. Shocks must provide proper damping force during rebound to control the springs. They must also possess enough compression to help the springs keep compliance with the road and maintain tire adhesion.

The first step to determining the proper shock is to know the spring rate you intend to install. Spring rate combined with suspension travel at actual ride height will assist you in selecting the right shocks/struts. Pay close attention to suspension travel. Inadequate travel will result in unpredictable handling and cause severe suspension damage. Putting a Civic in the weeds can easily cause the shocks and struts rods to bend and/or snap. When this happens you find out just how expensive cutting your springs can be. The final cost could be as much as five times the cost of purchasing correctly engineered springs and shocks/struts.

When selecting performance shocks, the place to start is with gas-pressurized models. Pressurization almost completely negates the effects of cavitation (foaming of the oil). Remember, shocks are heat-dissipating devices. Heat breaks down the oil-based fluid in shocks; therefore, when heat is reduced or deflected, shocks work in a more efficient manner. For more precise handling under varying conditions, adjustable shocks are the answer. Shocks such as Tokico's five-way-adjustable Illumina models can provide superior results on the street or on the track. The adjustable valve rate allows you to "dial in" the type of stiffness you want.

Okay, so you're going to install performance springs this month and can't afford performance shocks for another few weeks or months. How long can you go with the O.E. components? How do you know when to swap out your old shocks? Recognizing when to replace shocks is important. Shock absorbers wear out gradually and shock wear can go undetected until one day, out of the blue, the car seems unstable.

Worn shocks can display a number of characteristics—the most noticeable of which is fluid leaking. A leaking shock needs to be replaced immediately. When a shock is this far gone, don't even think about traveling any farther than necessary. Another key is a noisy shock or one that thumps when compressed. This is also a dangerous situation. When replacing a broken or leaking shock with more than 12,000 miles wear, you should also replace the shock on the other side of the suspension. This will help maintain handling balance.

To test shocks for wear, push down on the bumper or corner of the car and abruptly let it go. If the shock is worn or bad, the car will more than once bounce past the normal ride position. There are other key indications of worn shocks:

- Excessive body roll during cornering or lane changes.
- An unstable or floating motion.
- A harsh ride.
- Suspension bottoms out.
- Reduced control during breaking.
- Early tire wear.

There are several important factors to consider when shopping for performance shocks. In outward appearance several brands of shocks look the same. Many brands use similar casings and packaging; however, what's inside can be substantially different. The quality of materials and construction techniques are vital to a superior performance shock. It is highly advisable to research the internal components of each shock brand before forking over between $50-$120 per shock. Compare the piston, rod guide, seals and oil used. A good-looking casing means nothing if the product inside is of poor quality.

A good-quality shock will retail for a minimum of $65. Good-quality struts will retail for about $125. There are rebuildable strut

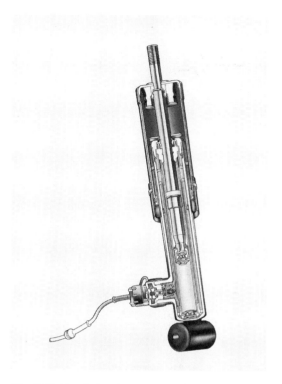

Fig. 3-13: Honda has been reported to be considering adding road-sensing suspension struts to its line. Commonly reserved for the upper-end brands, such as Acura, these items have the ability to receive feedback from the road surface and adjust their own valve rates and adapt to changing conditions.

cartridges, like the offerings from Doetsch Tech, that run about $85. As a general rule, the more expensive the shock the better the quality. Brand names like Koni, Tokico, Eibach and Bilstein are companies that engineer and market reliable shocks and struts and are safe bets when it comes to replacing O.E. or worn shocks.

By now you're saying enough with the shock treatment. It's true that up to this point there has been more information about shocks than springs. This shows how important shocks are to the handling and safe operation of your Civic. Consider one other fact: a lot of companies make springs but only a few make performance shocks. Narrowing the field down a bit further, only Tokico and Eibach offer both.

Good-quality shocks are more than a performance item; they're an investment in your Civic. Good performance shocks pay for themselves many times over during their lifetime. Improved cornering, better vehicle control, longer tire life and fewer trips to the hospital for kidney dialysis are all benefits of selecting good-quality performance shocks.

Bushings

From springs to shocks to bushings? Most enthusiasts figure the next logical installment in the suspension saga would be anti-roll or sway bars. Well, guess again. Before you can fully appreciate the potential of anti-roll bars, you must first examine how bushings play a part in allowing your other suspension components to perform at their optimum levels.

Honda uses rubber bushings for all its production cars. There are various reasons for this long-standing practice. Honda knows that the vast majority of Civic owners never intend to push the performance limits of their coupe, sedan or hatchback. But, more important, bushings made of rubber offer the most economical material choice. Rubber is a low-cost compound that efficiently absorbs vibration and does not require the fit to have close tolerances.

While rubber bushings respond well to common everyday driving conditions, these bushings have major shortcomings in performance applications. First and foremost, rubber bushings are more likely to become displaced during demanding driving. When severe cornering control is necessary, rubber bushings can cause suspension components to lose the precision geometry and render them less effective.

The second problem with rubber bushings is that over time they break down. With every mile, bump, curve and swerve, rubber bushings continue to deteriorate. Exposure to oil, gasoline, solvents, moisture, grit, dirt, sand, road debris, road salt and harsh weather compounds the rub-

ber's breakdown process. Depending on where each bushing is placed, within a few years your O.E. bushings can be transformed to be as hard as rocks or as mushy as half-baked pudding on a hot summer sidewalk.

Many race teams and sportsman racers have discovered polyurethane to be the answer. However, it comes with a price—or two. On the plus side, polyurethane is an extremely stable compound that is not affected by petroleum-based fluids or atmospheric contaminants. It can be formed in varying degrees of hardness, from toy-like slime to golfball hard. To achieve these or any level in between requires the product to be formed to exact tolerances. Polyurethane bushings perform better than rubber because they allow suspension movement through rotational sliding, realizing a more responsive suspension.

The downside to polyurethane bushings include a harsher, less comfortable ride and a noisy squeaking sound. The ride quality is affected because the bushings work so much better than the soft rubber factory counterparts. For all its disadvantages, rubber is superior to polyurethane in absorbing noise and transferring energy.

In the battle of performance, the pros of polyurethane win out over the cons. In fact, many performance suspension companies highly recommend the use of polyurethane bushings over rubber. Most include them as upgrades with anti-roll bars and shocks. Oh, yes—there is one more little factor to consider: polyurethane is cheaper than rubber. If you're restoring or rebuilding an older Civic, replacing all the rubber bushings on the car with polyurethane will cost less than $500. Installing the O.E. rubber components will run close to $750. What's more, polyurethane will never break down or wear out.

Anti-Roll Bars

The primary function of anti-roll bars is to assist in the overall control of the vehicle. Anti-roll bars tie two lower ends of the suspension together—in a sense making independent suspension less independent. In doing this, anti-roll bars perform the exact function they are named for—they reduce body roll.

Reducing body roll provides your Civic with one very important benefit: quicker transitional response. This rapidly brings the car back to point zero after encountering a corner or turn. By bringing the car back to point zero, the next corner can be attacked more aggressively and with far greater control. (Anti-roll bars, by the way, have no effect on the fore/aft pitch of the car.)

When setting up a race car, chassis experts try to achieve an ideal relationship between front and rear roll stiffness, better known as "roll couple." Anti-roll bars are the device used to accomplish perfect roll couple. Adjusting the vehicle's chassis balance is done through the use of springs and bars.

Anti-roll bar stiffness is determined by three factors: diameter, overall length and movement length. The larger in diameter the bar is, the greater the increase in roll stiffness. Stiffness can also be adjusted by shortening the movement length.

Honda Civics are factory-equipped with small-diameter front anti-roll bars. These are fine for everyday grandmas but do little or nothing when you flog the car around a road course. By replacing the 15mm or smaller bars with 20-25mm bars, ride quality stiffens and handling is vastly improved. And, if you've got the "build in subtraction" mode firmly entrenched, you should know that most good-quality anti-roll bars come with polyurethane bushings.

Strut Tower Bars

The upper strut tower bar is to the top of the suspension what an anti-roll bar is to the bottom of the suspension: it ties the upper strut towers together for increased stability and chassis stiffness.

Upper strut bars are quite simple in nature—they consist of a flat bar or diameter tube with fittings to secure the left and right sides of the chassis. The big difference is that this is done across the Civic's engine compartment. The strut towers

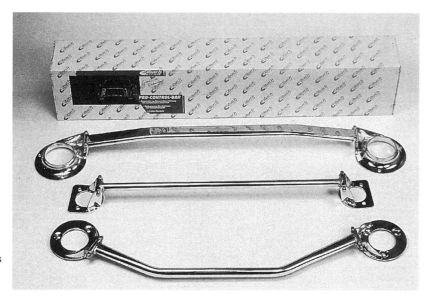

Fig. 3-14: An upper strut tie bar is a cost-effective way to gain suspension performance. Besides the improved handling, this is an item that looks good under the hood.

Fig. 3-15: Installing an upper strut tie bar requires a socket set and a coffee break. Simply remove the upper strut assembly nuts.

Fig. 3-16: Drop the tie bar in place, put the nuts back into place and tighten.

Fig. 3-17: To adjust the bar's pitch, use an open-end wrench and adjust the nuts on each end of the tie bar.

extend like a tunnel from the engine compartment through to the lower suspension components. Fasteners secure the strut/spring assembly at the top of this tunnel. The upper strut tie bar links the two struts together. The strut tower bar can be installed quickly and easily within a few minutes.

TIRES

Perhaps the most important part of any suspension upgrade is the tires. The size, tread type, speed rating and surface compound vary from brand to brand and from size or fitments. Stock, factory-issued tires provide a quiet, smooth ride with low-rolling resistance for healthy fuel economy and long

tread life. The compound is hard, which compromises superior handling for long life. This is fine if performance handling is not as important as comfort. Remember that these are tires that are made for the common Honda owner who never expects to push the envelope of the car.

Moving up in tire size and width will greatly benefit the handling of a Civic but will cost you a small amount of engine performance as well as fuel economy and tire life. The two main reasons for these compromises are higher rolling resistance and more aggressive driving.

The most common term you'll hear when it comes to tire fitment is "Plus." If you take the average factory-equipped Civic available over the past four years, you find the tire size to be 185/65-14. From this point you go to Plus One, Plus Two, Plus Three and in extreme cases, Plus Four. Each Plus gets bigger in section width size, and each size change alters the performance capabilities of the car. Some changes are slight, while others are noticeable. For example, with stock size tires, 0-60 times were better then a Plus Four fitment. But

Fig. 3-18: Tires are perhaps the most important element to the overall look and feel of your Civic. However, this is also an area where you can save some cash. While a "Z"-rated tire makes you look like a speed demon, it is highly unlikely you're going to achieve speeds in excess of 180 mile per hour. Therefore, you can spend a lot less to achieve the same performance results by buying a lower-speed-rated tire.

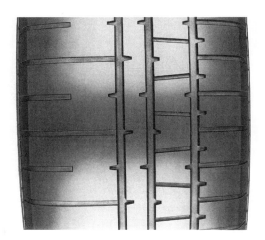

Fig. 3-19: B.F. Goodrich developed the Comp T/A R1 tire from technology acquired in motorsport competition. The R1 has an asymmetrical design engineered for wet-weather racing. Tread blocks on the outer edge of the tire are larger than those on the inside. This provides block stability, which is important for hard cornering.

Tests

ITEM	O.E.	PLUS ONE	PLUS TWO	PLUS THREE	PLUS FOUR
Tires	185/65-14	205/50-15	205/45-16	205/40-17	205/35-18
Wheel	14x5	15x7	16x7	17x7	18x7
Diameter.	23.5	23.1	23.3	23.5	23.7
0-60	9.3	9.5	9.3	9.3	9.5
1/4 mi.	17.1	17.3	17.3	17.2	17.3
MPH	82	81	82	82	82
Braking 60-0	146′	119′	127′	118′	119′
Skid pad "g"	0.72	0.86	0.84	0.87	0.89
Slalom course (in mph)	62.1	66.9	64.2	67.1	67.6
Db@ 60 mph	66	71	71	70	73

Summary

	1	2	3	4	5
Size	+4	+3	+2	+1	O.E.
Diameter	+4	+3	O.E.	+2	+1
0-60	+2	O.E.	+3	+1	+4
1/4 mile	O.E.	+3	+2	+4	+1
MPH	O.E.	+3	+4	+2	+1
Braking	+3	+4	+1	+2	O.E.
Skid Pad	+4	+3	+1	+2	O.E.
Slalom	+4	+3	+1	+2	O.E.
Quiet	O.E.	+3	+1	+2	+4
Weight	+2	+3	O.E.	+1	+4
Appearance	+3	+2	+4	+1	O.E.
Cost	O.E.	+2	+1	+3	+4

the factory size gives away 27 feet in braking distance and over five miles per hour in the 600-foot slalom test. Using this simple theory, you'd think that the larger the tire size the better the performance. However, tests show that this is not always the case. Check out the driving test results above. (All tests were conducted on a 1997 Civic Ex coupe. Tires were Toyo brand on TSW wheels.)

OVERALL RATINGS

First Choice: Plus Three. The ideal blend of performance and appearance. The tire side-wall and wheel alloy mass provide the right amount of wheel well clearance and visual appeal. For performance, braking is superior to all the combos tested and this fitment ranked second in quarter-mile time and miles per hour, skid pad and slalom course. This size also offered an acceptable on-ramp acceleration and only scored poorly in cost (about $1,500 for the set of four tires and wheels).

Second Choice: Plus Four. Okay, we can't resist the massive amount of wheel wrapped around a rubber band of tire. While you give up ride quality and quiet you get a handling factor that ranks high in slalom and skid pad.

This is due to the rigidity of the sidewall (or lack of it). The major cosmetic problem with 18-inch wheels is that 17-inch tires and wheels fit the dimensions of the Civic body far better.

Third Choice: Plus Two. A set of 16-inch tires and wheels are a good conservative choice. Offered in many contemporary styles, a set of wheels you like won't be hard to find. The downside is the high possibility of buyer remorse. That's right—you buy the 16s and end up three months later wanting to move up to 17s. (See "building through subtraction" in Chapter 2.)

Fourth Choice: O.E. Believe it or not, if you're going to waste the money on a set of 15-inch tires and wheels, you might as well keep the factory tread and steel wheels. Save your money until the factory tires run down to the wear bars, then step up to a Plus Three setup.

Enough with all this talk of rankings and ratings. Let's get to the right tire setup for maximum handling. Truth be known, it all comes down to the contact patch—that small portion of the tread that actually meets the driving surface. On a dry road a wider contact patch usually equals better road adhesion. However, when the weather turns nasty, wide tires can cause a greater risk of hydroplaning. This is where a thinner tread can be an advantage.

Most performance tires are offered with a continuous tread pattern, and on wet surfaces the bigger contact patch encounters more water. The tread does not have the capacity to clear away this amount of water before the plane between the two is compromised and loss of traction occurs. Some tiremakers are engineering their brands with tread designed to look like two separate tires fused in the middle. This allows for a wide-tread tire to act like two smaller tires on slick, wet roads. On dry pavement, the fat contact patch provides superior handling. Thus, the best of both worlds.

Wheels

While wheels have little or nothing to do with handling, there are a number of factors to consider before jacking up the car and yanking off the factory issues for new alloy and rubber. The first thing to take into account is the style of wheels you want. Rim or rimless (also called "softline")? Rivets/fasteners or smooth face? Aluminum or steel? Forged one piece, two piece or three piece? What about weight, durability and DOT approval? There's a lot more to think about than just style.

Everyone has an individual idea of styling, so you can address that issue with your inner voice. As for the rest of the list, that's a different story. The material used in the making of each wheel is critical to its quality. Before selecting the brand of wheels you want, look closely at the casting. Check the display wheel for smooth, consistent material flow, especially on the inner rim of the wheel.

Wheels are made in many different countries: United States, Mexico, Germany, South Africa, the Philippines, Japan, Taiwan, Korea, China, Italy, Great Britain, etc. Some countries have varying levels of materials available. One good way to determine the quality in manufacturing is by the amount of counterweights needed to balance the tires and wheels. If you can convince your local tire and wheel dealer to submit each considered wheel to a spin balance test, you'll see what counter-balance weight is all about. The test is quite simple: mount only the wheel on the spin balance machine, start the machine and record the amount of weight needed to bring the wheel to dead-center balance. You do this without mounting the wheels to the tires to avoid the factor of each tire having its own balance problems.

For performance enthusiasts, weight should be a major factor. Wheels that look alike may be made thousands of miles apart, using different manufacturing methods and with different grades of material. For exam-

Putting the Two Together

WHEEL SIZE	OFFSET	TIRE SIZE
14x6	35-38	185/60-14
14x7	35	185/60-14
15x7	35	195/50-15
15x7	38	205/50-15
16x7	35	205/45-16
16x7	35	205/40-16
17x7	35	205/45/17
17x7	35	205/40-17
18x7	35-38	205/35/18

ple, a TSW Stealth wheel is a five-star wheel that is several pounds heavier than a JM Motorsports JM5 wheel. Although both are 17-inch cast aluminum five-star wheels and have DOT approval, the way they are designed and manufactured make them vastly different. When you're gutting the car to shed it of unwanted pounds, it makes sense to select wheels that are lighter in weight yet retain a high level of strength and integri-

ty. To the left is a chart to determine quickly and easily the tire and wheel setup for your Civic, CRX or del Sol, using bolt pattern 4x100.

Traction Reaction

Thus far, the road has taken us from boring factory stock to street machine. What about special needs, like road racing or sportsman class? And let's not forget drag racing. What about these areas of suspension technology?

Import drag racing is the fastest growing participation sport in America. Each month hundreds of new sportsman-class drivers try their hands at screaming down the 1320 pavement (1,320 feet equals 1/4 mile). While this form of racing offers its own special engine performance requirements, setting up a Civic's suspension to gain maximum traction is vastly different from rear-wheel drive cars.

Fig. 3-20: For front-wheel-drive drag racing, the suspension logic is reversed from that of rear wheel drive cars. For Civic, CRX and del Sol models, weight transfer needs to be eliminated, keeping downforce on the front wheels.

In rear-wheel drive applications, weight is naturally transferred from the front of the car to the rear. As acceleration takes place, the force of power over gravity takes over, sending downforce to the rear-drive wheels. The front of the car lifts until the power is relieved during transmission shift changes. At that time, the front dives as torque is momentarily lost. To keep weight transfer to the rear tires, special shocks and springs have been developed to assist in optimum weight transfer. In front-wheel drive cars, such as the Civic and CRX, the exact opposite action is needed. Instead of the weight being transferred to rear of the car, it must be retained over the front wheels. Traditional theories of traction and weight transfer thus do not apply.

The first step in setting up your Civic suspension for drag racing goes against logic. Earlier, we talked about the importance of anti-roll bars for improved handling. When you get to the drag strip, which is straight (or is supposed to be), the anti-roll bar is an item that is no longer needed. By removing the front anti-roll bar, the independent front suspension is allowed to work in an independent manner. This is easy to understand when you remember one of the basic laws of nature: for every action there is an equal and opposite reaction. As the driving tire gains adhesion to the pavement, its natural downforce delivers an opposite lifting force. This action causes this side to lose traction and control. The downforce also wants to transfer energy to the rear of the car, where it has no appreciable effect on performance. The key is to keep the weight transfer from taking place.

A number of years ago Eibach Springs developed the first Drag Launch springs for Honda Civics. What makes these springs special is the unique rate engineered into the springs. These springs have a rebound factor that helps keep the car front lifting on sudden acceleration. By getting the nose of the car to squat, weight transfer is minimized and traction is retained.

Another suspension stance trick for drag racing is to raise the rear suspension of the Civic to force the weight transfer to remain over the front wheels. This can be accomplished by replacing the rear shocks with hard bars after arriving at the track. These bars are simple straight steel bars with shock-mount fittings. When in place, these bars prevent rear weight transfer because the car has no rear suspension damping ability. A word of caution: hard bars should never be used on the street; in fact, none of the suspension techniques used to improve drag racing performance are advised for any form of street use.

Coil-Over Springs

One of the most misunderstood and financially wasteful suspension items is coil-over

Fig. 3-21: It may be overkill for the street, but coil-over springs and struts represent the best formula for controlling ride height and stiffness for varying conditions and needs.

springs. Coil-over springs packages are coil springs on struts that feature threaded adjustments. This adjustment allows you to dial in the amount of stiffness and lowering to accommodate different needs. What has made this wasteful is two-fold. First, properly designed coil-over springs kits can cost from $750-$1,500. That's a ton of cash if you never intend to use the kit to its full competition potential. Second, most street car Civic owners simply want coil-over springs because it is believed the car can be correctly lowered with these kits.

Whether you're using coil springs or coil-over kits, the basic laws of suspension geometry apply. Lower is not always better. So when are coil-over springs useful? Coil-overs are ideal for multifunction users. For daily street driving, a one-or-two inch suspension drop is perfect: it supplies good ride quality and excellent handling. For Solo racing, you can turn down the spring/strut combo to achieve stiffer suspension tension. If the race track features multilevel surfaces with reverse-curve banking and varying road surfaces, coil-overs can be adjusted to height and stiffness levels that are right for the track.

If you absolutely must have coil-over springs, research the brands carefully. When selecting suspension components, don't look to save a few bucks at the expense of quality. Trust me—you'll be sorry. Springs are a quality-sensitive product. Not only should the spring rates be precisely engineered, but the steel material used should be of the highest quality. This goes double for coil-over springs. With the correct rating and highest-quality materials, the final cost will be substantially more then just repairing tweaked suspension parts.

Summary

Suspension modifications are the heart and soul of your Civic project. Achieving the right stance combined with pleasing tire and wheel selections can make or break the rest of the project. This is the exterior appearance you will be judged by. If your Civic, CRX or del Sol looks, drives and handles with high levels of approval, you have the correct foundation. The optimum goal is quality. Search out the best quality in products. If you can't afford the best, find a reasonable second choice. DON'T BUY BY PRICE—BUY BY QUALITY. If you know you want the best products but have to wait an extra month to afford them, it's far wiser to wait those extra 30 days than spend hundreds of dollars later in the project to replace lesser-quality springs, shocks, bars or bushings. Remember, the satisfaction of a quality product lasts long after the excitement of a low price.

Bolt-On Performance

Fig. 4-1: The most common bolt-on performance items include air intake systems, headers, cam gears, plugs, wires and coils.

A few weeks have passed since you dropped the stance of your Civic. You're taking full advantage of the improved handling by turning every on-ramp into a g-force challenge. But that sticky road feel has robbed your small in-line four-cylinder engine of throttle response. The problem is the greater tire tread surface you're demanding the de-tuned engine to pull around. It's time to locate the hood release and reclaim that lost performance.

There are many bolt-on ways to get back the throttle action. When you use the term "bolt-on" it should mean just that—bolt on. Some import performance manufacturers claim to offer products that improve horsepower and are simple to install. However, when it comes to the bolt-on distinction, it's buyer beware. Before purchasing any performance component, research the manufacturer's reputation and track record.

This can be done in a variety of ways. First, look through leading monthly import performance publications, such as *Sport Compact Car, Super Street* and *Hot Compact & Imports* magazines. These magazines often run stories, reviews and testing results. However, because magazines are really in the business of selling advertising space, rarely are the editors allowed to reveal negative results. In most cases, if a product doesn't perform well in magazine tests, the product is not talked about, or it is left out of the comparison-testing.

The next best source is other Honda owners. Ask other Civic/CRX/del Sol owners to be honest about the products they have selected for their cars. The friendly counter salesperson at your local tuner or speed shop can also be a good source. The downside to counter salespeople is

Untangling the mind-boggling information of ignition wires, cold air intakes, exhaust systems, cam timing, headers, pulleys, and ECU units. Do you really need all this stuff? Read on, my Honda brother.

41

that they are in the store to sell product and may not have all the product choices you need to make the best decision. Last, go back to those leading publications and read the feature and project vehicle stories. This will give you a good understanding what other Honda owners are installing. The bottom line is to seek out a number of sources before making your bolt-on product selection.

So just what exactly is a bolt-on performance product? The true definition of "bolt-on performance product" is a product that requires

- No modification of existing components
- No cutting, welding or torching
- No special tools
- Limited installation time
- Delivery of actual horsepower gains

To meet these five requirements, some manufacturers use creative terminology to convince you its product lives up to the bolt-on category. While this chapter explores the six basic performance food groups, it can't warn you of all the pitfalls of poorly designed product brands and applications. It will, however, provide you with a good understanding of what bolt-on performance products can do and how you can become an educated enthusiast.

The six areas of bolt-on performance discussed in this chapter are

- Air induction systems
- Cam timing and overdrive pulleys
- Headers vs. stock exhaust
- Performance exhaust systems
- Power ignition
- ECU (on-board computers)

These topics are the foundation for the more elaborate modifications to be described later in the book. Each topic features techniques to add from 3-15 horsepower. Each is designed to set your budget back less than $500. All the products can be found over the counter. And, most important, they do not

require you to open any vital internal area of your car's engine. Every item can be installed in your garage in less than a day using common tools and minimal preparation or formal education.

To make prioritizing easy, start with the products that are most likely to deliver the horsepower gains. It is wise to examine the claims of all the products in any category before making a purchase. Investigate the ease of installation and the time required to install each item. Always allow twice as much time to complete the job as advertised. This will ensure that you will have enough time to perform the task in a relaxed manner. This also allows the unexpected to be expected, such as a run or two to the local auto parts store for items that may not survive the install (belts, clamps, etc.) or may get misplaced (nuts, bolts, fasteners, etc).

Before beginning any install—bolt-on or otherwise—here are a few common items to have on hand

- Soft blankets or towels (to cover the exterior fenders)
- Spray lubricant such as WD-40 (to loosen frozen nuts, bolts, screws and fasteners)
- Masking tape (to temporarily secure items out of the way)
- Zip ties (to reroute and secure lines and hoses)
- Golf tees (to cap off vacuum lines)
- Black spray paint (to touch up areas)
- Shop rags (to clean areas and any fluid leaks or spills)
- Hand cleaner (to keep your hands clean. You can't put an engine together with dirt)
- Note pad and pencil (to remind yourself of locations of items)
- Grease pencil (to mark the locations of lines, hoses and other components)

Enough said. It's time to pop the hood release and get started.

Air Induction Systems

The most hyped products on the market are air induction systems. Dozens of manufacturers offer these pipe and filter products. Some make wild claims of massive horsepower gains. Some just look like performance is built in, while others actually are designed to make your Civic, CRX or del Sol perform with greater horsepower, torque and economy.

The function of a performance air induction system is to increase airflow capacity and velocity and deliver colder air to the fuel injectors. Some brands use one or two of these elements; only a few combine all three. The trick is to discover the system that will fit under your hood and within your budget.

The original equipment air filtration device is a more efficient delivery system than some aftermarket items. However, when asked to perform at higher engine rpm over extended periods of time, its operation becomes limiting. The paper filter Honda installs does not offer adequate airflow to optimize performance. In more recent models, the location of the inlet is well positioned to grab cooler outside air. Delivering cool air to the fuel injectors or carburetor is the most important function of the air induction system—factory or performance.

The deliverance of cooler or even cold air is the primary reason to install an aftermarket component. The cooler the air, the more dense the air/fuel mixture. A dense mixture means more fuel can be compressed into the cylinder. The greater the fuel compression, the more violent the ignition. The more violent the ignition, the greater the force with which the piston is driven. Greater piston drive force equals more useable power.

Performance aftermarket air induction systems were originally developed to grab cooler air, preferably from outside the engine compartment, and transport it through a more efficient filter and larger pipe to the fuel injectors. However, over the short evolution of this product, many manufacturers of these systems have lost sight of the primary goal.

Fig. 4-2: In long or short air intake systems, one of the keys to air velocity is the filter design. The cutaway design shows a sophisticated air horn or funnel shape when it directs air into the pipe.

Working with convoluted ideas and goals, manufacturers have created systems that are nothing more than fancy looking tubes with mushroom-shaped filter elements.

So how do you tell the contenders from the pretenders? Here are a few important tips: Aftermarket air induction systems are separated into three categories: (1) short pipe, (2) long pipe and (3) competition. All three allow for a greater airflow capacity. Two allow for cooler airflow. All three look better than the factory air box and plastic tubing. So now is the time to decide what's important—appearance or power? Or, throwing a wrench into the works, can you have both?

Short Pipes

There are dozens of short-pipe air induction systems available. Most offer superior appearance but deliver only minimal or no performance gains. This is because the materials used cannot compensate for the hot air that is forced into the system. Short pipes draw air from within the engine compartment, the warmest place in your Honda. Temperatures quickly reach the boiling point within minutes, even on a cold day. This air, while good for quickly warming the engine during cold-climate operation, sucks (pun intended) when it comes to making horsepower.

Of the three vital factors that make air induction systems successful, most short-pipe systems deliver only one: airflow capacity. Most short-pipe systems are made from three-inch pipes and are fitted with a popular style of air filter element. While more airflow capacity is a good thing, this effect is negated by air temperature. In fact, in some systems, the air capacity works against the performance process. This happens because heat rises. When the hot air reaches the turn in the pipe, it wants to fill only the top half of the pipe, leaving the bottom of the pipe to waste. Therefore, the increased capacity is only used when the pipe is straight. As soon as the air reaches the turn of the pipe, less than the entire pipe capacity is used and a blockage of air can occur. Add to this the increased heat and you've got no noticeable difference over the factory air intake.

More important than air capacity is air velocity. This is especially critical in short-pipe systems. The faster the air can get from the filter element to the fuel injectors the less heat it is exposed to, thus better density. Only a few manufacturers have discovered the benefits of smaller pipe diameter to increase airflow velocity. Airflow velocity can also eliminate the blockage or heat rise at the pipe turn. This is accomplished by rapidly forcing the air to the injectors. What helps take away the heat-rise problem to an even greater extent is the use of a split chamber at the pipe turn. However, because no manufacturer offers this feature, it is one you must perform yourself.

Coatings and finish also play a big part in the performance aspect of air induction systems. While polished and chrome finishes look cool, they are anything but. Chrome plating acts like a blanket, trapping heat inside and absorbing even more heat from the outside. This results in far less air density and reduces horsepower potential. Therefore, for show, chrome is ideal; for performance, it just doesn't work.

This leads us to polished aluminum intake pipes. These look great and offer better heat resistance than chrome. However, polished pipes require constant attention and care to maintain a show-

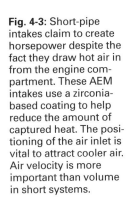
Fig. 4-3: Short-pipe intakes claim to create horsepower despite the fact they draw hot air in from the engine compartment. These AEM intakes use a zirconia-based coating to help reduce the amount of captured heat. The positioning of the air inlet is vital to attract cooler air. Air velocity is more important than volume in short systems.

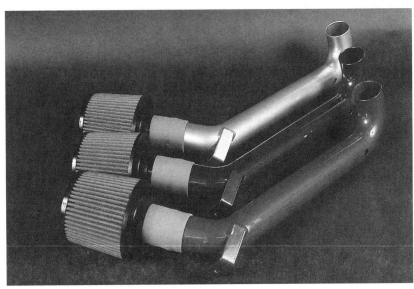

quality appearance. Color-anodized pipes deliver appearance and performance qualities because the anodizing absorbs less heat than the bare aluminum pipes.

The best for both appearance and performance is powder coating, especially when a zirconia-based coating is used. Zirconia prevents heat penetration, greatly reducing the air temperature. Only one manufacturer, AEM, offers its short-pipe systems with zirconia-based powder coating, because of the extra expense needed for this process.

No short-pipe system can be called a cold-air system; rather it is a "performance air intake." The average short-pipe system will net four horsepower and requires about two hours to complete the install. The average price is $199.

Long Pipes

Long-pipe systems can honestly carry the title of "cold-air induction" because they offer the opportunity to claim air from outside the engine compartment. However, some systems require a little modification of inner fender wells or grill areas to achieve true cold-air status. Some are designed to fit neatly between the radiator mountings and headlight buckets, routing down under the car to a place where cooler air is available.

Like the short-pipe systems, long-pipe units must carry the air from the filter to the injectors passing through the engine compartment. As mentioned in the last section, the engine compartment gets extremely hot, thus the challenge of keeping the air moving quickly enough to not absorb this heat. Once again the finish of the pipe plays a big part in determining the air delivery temperature.

There are many true long-pipe systems on the market. The Iceman system features a unique molded pipe with a funnel effect to speed up air velocity. AEM's cold air induction product features a heat resistant zirconia powder-coated pipe in a slightly smaller diameter, which increases airflow velocity.

Both have been dyno proven to deliver substantial horsepower gains—in some cases as much as 15 horsepower.

Because long-pipe systems from Iceman, AEM, HKS and others all deliver measurable horsepower, the trick is to find the one unit that can supply the most. One way to separate the men from the boys is the type of filter used. Each manufacturer has its own special theory on how one is better than another. RS Akimoto and AEM use filter elements with funnel ram devices to increase airflow velocity at the entry point. Other makers use a long K&N cone-style filter with improved air capacity. In testing 1988-99 Civics, velocity wins the horsepower war over capacity.

The final word on both short- and long-pipe systems is the street-legal issue. If state or local mandates affect the registration of your Civic, you may want to be sure the air intake system is C.A.R.B.-certified before making the purchase. The C.A.R.B. (California Air Resource Board) standard is the standard that most other states follow. Intakes that have passed C.A.R.B testing and

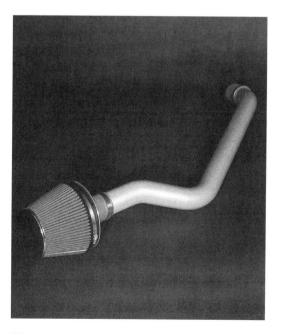

Fig. 4-4: Long-pipe systems can truly be called cold-air induction systems. However, as with its short-pipe counterpart, it is air velocity that makes the difference, not air volume.

are certified will have a C.A.R.B. number imprinted on the pipe.

The average long-pipe system will net nine horsepower and requires about three hours to complete the install. The average price is $249.

Competition

Competition air intake systems do not really fall within the bolt-on category, but since we're in the neighborhood we might as well pay a visit. These systems can range from exotic filters to nothing more than further extensions of a long-pipe system. While philosophies vary, one thing is consistent: none of these systems is truly street-legal.

There are three basic varieties of competition systems—above, below and in front. Above systems grab air from over the hood line, much like air scoops installed on vintage domestic muscle cars. These systems require either the use of a special hood or modification of your stock hood. Because the pipe is short, this style features rapidly forced air and quick delivery. Heat-rise problems are all but eliminated because the air flows so quickly for such a short distance that the incoming air never has a chance to heat up.

Below systems require the pipe and filter combination to grab air from under the car. This entry placement provides the coolest air possible, but it has its limitations. For one, a good filter guard or grate is needed to protect the filter element damage from road debris and speed bumps. It also makes it necessary to elevate the car in order to change or inspect the filter. As with the above-hood system, heat is not a problem because the pipe is located a fair distance from the heat-causing components of the engine.

A good up-front system is no more than an extension of a long-pipe system. However, there is a twist for up-front advocates. In 1997 Knight Engineering introduced the Iceman Ram Air System, a clever and cost-effective device that replaces the right headlight assembly with a molded air funnel. This device can be used with an Iceman or most other air intake systems or even the factory air pipe. A word of caution: this air funnel does not allow for an air filter. While Iceman includes a screen to catch unwanted debris, the absence of a filter and the non-street-legal configuration of only one headlight makes this a track-only product.

An old trick from the street racers of the 1970s is to inject a little "arctic freeze" into your air system. This requires installing a

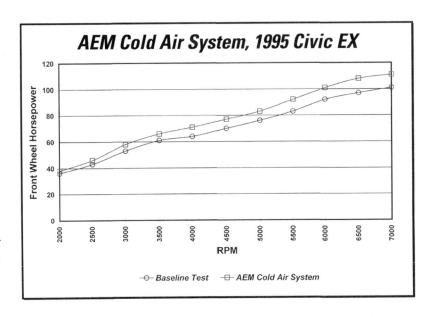

Fig. 4-5: On an average Civic (in this case a '95 EX coupe) a long-pipe system can start to deliver noticeable horsepower gains beginning at 3,000 rpm. By the time you approach the top of the powerband you can feel the 10 extra horsepower.

"cold box" onto your air pipe. The cold box is nothing more than an aluminum canister that the air pipe runs through. You drop a small block of dry ice inside the canister just before racing. This supercools the air before it reaches the injectors. A similar and easier effect can be accomplished by routing your fuel line through a cold box. However, be aware that this may cause a massive temporary horsepower surge and should not be combined with the use of nitrous oxide.

All in all, a good air induction system can net significant horsepower gains. For the money, this may be the most cost-effective way to increase horsepower for small Civic/CRX and del Sol engines.

Cam Timing and Overdrive Pulleys

Over the past few years cam timing gears have become the rage among Honda tuners. While these precision products certainly look the performance part, in most SOHC engines cam timing can yield only minor results. However, in Honda twin cam VTEC engines, cam timing can be very rewarding.

Cam timing tricks are in no way a new method of gaining performance. The fact that this method has stood the test of time is a testament to the fact that adjustable cam gears work—but not without a trade-off.

Adjusting the valve timing allows you to dial in the camshaft power band for low-end power (power made at the bottom end of the rpm range) or increased top end. But on single cam engines you must choose because you can't have it both ways at the same time. On twin cam engines adjustments can be made in combinations. This is both a blessing and a curse because tuning becomes far more complicated.

Adjustable cam gears do not change the cam's lift or duration. What they do is change the opening and closing of valves, thus changing the performance output of the engine. By advancing the gears you increase low-end power but by retarding the

Dyno Test w/ AEM Cold Air Intake 1999 Civic Si VTEC

RPM RANGE	FACTORY HORSEPOWER	UPGRADED HORSEPOWER
1500	8.7	9.0
1750	77	79
2000	90	92
2500	113	117
3000	148	152
3500	153	159
4000	157	162
4500	165	170
5000	169	174
5500	174	180

timing you better the top-end or high rpm power. In simple terms, if you were going to require your Honda powerplant to deliver performance between 85-110 miles per hour in the rpm range of plus 3,500 for an extended period of time, you would retard the timing. When greater torque at lower rpm is needed, advance the timing. However, all timing modifications should be done with caution. Do not fall into the "if a little is good, more must be better" trap. Adjusting the valve timing can be an exact science—for those who know how to do it and have the right equipment (chassis dyno) to perform a proper dial-in procedure.

Fig. 4-6: Cam timing gears can be useful in tuning torque. Most Civics have SOHC engines, which severely limit the effectiveness of these items. For DOHC Honda powerplants, the results can be much greater.

What makes gaining horsepower from twin cam engines so much easier is the fact that intake and exhaust valves can be set independently. On single cam engines the degree of both intake and exhaust is done from one adjustment. While a twin cam engine is nice to have, the vast majority of Civic owners find themselves modifying the tried and true single cam. This is by no means a bad thing; in fact it can be very good. Sure, the twin cam VTEC engine is the hot ticket, but the single cam is far less demanding when it comes to cam timing. The cold hard truth is that 90 percent of all twin cam VTEC owners who install adjustable cam gears never take them off the dead-zero settings, usually for fear of never getting the two valve sets to work in harmony in a combination of advancing and retarding.

To give you a better idea of the degree of performance gain you can expect by adjusting the cam timing gear(s), the following chart shows the dyno recap of a Honda DOHC (non-VTEC) engine.

While cam-timing gear(s) help maximize power, they do nothing without being set correctly. You should select a timing gear on one basic factor: quality. A good adjustable cam gear will offer features that make installation and cam adjustments easy and will deliver a high level of reliability and dependability. The first factor is easy-adjustment hardware, such as allen head or metric socket adjustment bolts that can quickly and easily be loosened and secured. Next look for simple-to-read adjustment markings, which should be etched into the cam gear face. It is best to have the markings on the extreme face of the gear, closest to the belt surface. Precise teeth castings are vital to ensure consistent belt tension. All the teeth should be exactly alike and should fit the timing belt as Honda intended. To guarantee ideal operation throughout the rpm range, insist on using only cam gear(s) with a hard-anodized belt surface. Without a durable belt surface, the teeth may shear off,

causing the timing belt to become detached and result in a total shutdown of power.

Installing cam-timing gear(s) is really straightforward. To start, disconnect your battery to ensure the engine starter has no electrical power source. Next, set the number-one piston to top dead center (TDC). This makes removing and installing the cam gear(s) much easier.

Remove the cam cover and ignition wires. Now you have a good view of the stock cam gear(s). By removing the front engine cover you have access to the cam gear(s). Before you get headstrong and remove the stock cam gear(s), however, first loosen the timing belt tensioner. There is a key tab on the cam, which you can see when you look at the center of the cam gear. This should be at the top position, indicating the engine is at TDC. (This is where the engine should be before you remove the cam gear(s).) After you remove the stock cam gear(s), the front of the engine appears barren. This is a good time to remember you can't put an engine together with dirt. Now it is just a matter of installing the adjustable cam gear(s) and attaching the belt. Before securing, consult a Honda maintenance manual for tensioner specifications.

Many Honda Civic owners do not reinstall the factory front cam gear cover because some aftermarket adjustable cam gear(s) look as good as they work. This makes

Charting DOHC Power

RPM	DEAD ZERO	THREE-DEGREE RETARD
2,000	41	42
2,500	47	54
3,000	53	65
3,500	64	72
4,000	72	81
4,500	81	91
5,000	90	99
5,500	99	106
6,000	105	124
6,500	121	131
7,000	126	133

adjustable cam-timing gears a little bit show and a little bit go.

The average cam timing gear set will run $199 and will yield six to nine horsepower.

The perfect complements to adjustable cam-timing gear(s) are overdrive pulleys, which slow down the function of the device to which they are attached. By slowing down the operation of the air conditioning, power steering and (in some cases) the smog pump, you reduce the power needed to run them. This power can be used to drive the front wheels. Most pulley kits supply only a few horsepower, but in many cases two or three ponies equals the difference between winning and losing.

Overdrive pulleys are true bolt-on accessories. Easy to attach, the only trick is to ensure the pulley has the proper belt. Because the power-saving pulley is larger in diameter, stock belts will be too small to fit around the crank and accessory pulleys. Some pulley kits come complete with the proper belts. If the pulleys you use come without belts, measure the distance around the lower engine pulley and the entire route the belt must take with the new performance pulleys in place. Note the groove cut of the factory belt and then it's off to the parts store for a matching belt.

While installing performance pulleys you'll scrape the knuckles a bit because space is tight. But, like the adjustable cam gear(s), performance pulleys can provide more than a few extra horsepower, and they look good as well.

Performance pulley kits can run from $159 to $199 and deliver two to four horsepower.

Headers vs. Stock Exhaust

Almost every performance freak in America somehow from birth believes headers allow a car to go faster. Perhaps this is because the car geek gene is passed down from one generation to another. However, if you are one of these lucky people, you probably were

Fig. 4-7: A simple pulley kit can yield two to three extra horsepower. A complete kit should include properly sized belts.

exposed to V8 engines—and everyone knows V8 engines need headers to make horsepower.

In Honda engines the factory engineers did a masterful job in coming up with an exhaust manifold that delivers excellent power and torque throughout the powerband. This is not to say there is no room for improvement; it's just the improvement is not as drastic and neck-snapping as header manufacturers want you to believe.

To fully understand how a header works, you should know the primary function of the exhaust manifold. The practical theory is both simple and complex. Exhaust velocity is the key to making horsepower. (If you've been paying attention, this sounds familiar.) Velocity is also the key to performance induction systems. This is also the case when you need to get the bad air out.

A performance header is designed to draw and flow burned gases out of the combustion chamber in a quicker, more efficient manner, and exhaust extraction is a method used to help. When the exhaust valve opens, the upstroke of the piston pushes the burned gases out of the chamber through the exhaust valve. To help create a suction effect, the intake valve opens just before the exhaust valve fully closes. This sucks the fresh air/fuel mixture into the chamber and helps create a more volatile compression mixture. The negative turning point is when the exhaust manifold can't accommodate the flow of spent gases.

A well-engineered header offers improved exhaust flow by creating more powerful evacuation and greater flow capacity. It is the common belief that simply using a larger-diameter tube can increase flow. Tube size, however, is not always the most important factor. In addition to size, you must also factor in collector design and type as well as tube length.

There are two common Honda header designs, four-tube and Tri-Y. The two designs share benefits, but each is engineered to deliver different horsepower usage.

The four-tube design routes gases from four tubes to a single collector. There are a dozen brands available in a wide range of prices. On the entry end of the scale are steel tube headers that are crimp-bent. More effective are ceramic-coated aluminum models designed with four equal-length pipes

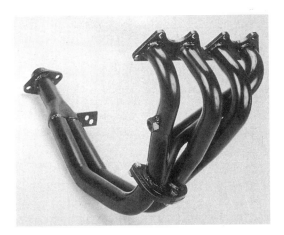

Fig. 4-8: An exhaust header should be a no-brainer when it comes to performance. However, be sure you're picking the right design for the type of performance you want.

that are mandrel-bent. These are lightweight and offer improved exhaust flow because the gases flow unobstructed to the collector. Four-tube headers are ideal for mid-to-high rpm engine operation, such as road-racing or rockin' the highway in third gear.

Tri-Y headers are designed to pair cylinders together to promote shared exhaust evacuation. Here, two pairs of tubes mix gases before reaching the collector. This results in low- to mid-range power. If you are looking to increase standing start torque (or city street power) this is a better choice.

On contemporary Civics, the factory exhaust manifold offers a well-engineered compromise between four-tube and Tri-Y headers, which is why many Civic builders feel little or no difference when a header is installed. Sure, aftermarket headers offer the appearance and tone of performance but don't always deliver the massive horsepower gains you expect.

When building a Civic for racing purposes, you must determine the most typical style of competition you will be involved in. For example, on a road course you will find greater use of power in the mid-to-high rpm range because you are shifting up and down through the gears more as you enter and exit turns and straightaways. You will want to keep the higher rpm range, allowing the engine to help decelerate as well as accelerate the car. For this reason you want to use a four-tube header. For drag racing, where most races are won or lost from a standing start, a Tri-Y header design has the advantage over the four-tube model. On short autocross circuits a Tri-Y header works the low- to mid-torque range with better response. This will allow you to work first and second gear more effectively in the tighter turns. You'll give up a little on the straight, but 95 percent of autocross circuits consist of quick right and left turns.

If you decide to install a header, you will be removing not only the Honda factory exhaust manifold but also the heat shield that goes with it. This is another small detail most Civic, CRX and del Sol owners overlook when trying to make horsepower. Even though it looks about as attractive as a wart on a covergirl's face, the factory heat shield serves a vital function. An exhaust manifold carries a tremendous amount of heat—in fact, it is the hottest component on your entire car. The factory heat shield helps deflect this heat away from the air intake. When a header replaces the factory exhaust manifold, most young performance seekers don't think about the heat that is now free to raise the air intake temperature. The result is loss of horsepower and throttle response in place of improved performance. To compensate for the greater heat problem, use a header tube wrap to cover the pipes, a trick used as far back as 35 years ago by road race teams and drag racers. Once again, if you've been paying attention to the addition-subtraction theory, you'll save the money of buying a chrome-plated header and opt instead for the white or black painted models because you'll be covering the header in heat wrap—or spend the extra dough and step up to the ceramic-coated header.

If it's the show-quality finish you're looking for, chrome plating can supply you with show points. Here's a simple step to help prevent the chrome from discoloring due to the extreme heat caused by the exhaust gases. Before installing the header, spray the inside of the pipes with a heat paint, such as VHT. And don't just spray a little in each pipe, use an entire can. To do this, start with a fresh header. Mask off the external areas around the collector and mounting surface. Hang the header in a way to make it easy to spray the paint directly into the ports. Spray about one-fourth of a can into each pipe. Let this set for about an hour before rehanging the header into a position where you will be spraying into the collector. Once again spray about one-fourth of a can of the heat paint into the header. Let this set for about two hours. Hang the header so you can spray into the ports and repeat the first spraying.

When you have finished, let the header set for a few days to ensure proper curing. Don't be impatient to install the header. Even though the paint can says the finish will dry in hours, letting the paint set up for a longer period of time won't hurt the process—trust me. While coating the interior of the header will not completely guard against chrome discoloration, it will slow the process down.

For the most part, a header will make you feel faster. If you choose the right exhaust manifold or header, chances are you will achieve some higher level of performance. Just be aware that in and of itself, a header will bring only modest gains. To have any advantage in a header, it must be combined with a performance exhaust system. This, however, is an entirely different subject.

An average header runs about $225.

Performance Exhaust Systems

Since I've brought up the subject, we might as well dispel the myths and hyped facts about bolt-on exhaust systems. Bolt-on exhaust systems do one thing extremely well—they deliver the sound of performance. That is not to say that all systems only sound good; some actually add performance. However, like all performance products, you should be on guard against items that can't live up to their claims.

Of all bolt-on products, exhaust systems give consumers the greatest amount of hype and deliver the least amount of return. This is not for lack of trying but more a misunderstanding of how a performance exhaust system works. On a recent test day several name-brand systems were installed on the same Civic EX coupe. All claimed big horsepower gains. All added to the performance exhaust tone. Every system offered a cool-looking tip. Some added unwanted sound resonance back through the system. Only two actually provided measurable as advertised horsepower.

Before installation, each system was examined by Ed Hanson, a noted performance exhaust expert. Experienced in developing exhaust systems for racing applications, he graded each system on ease of installation, component quality and system engineering. "It's little wonder some aftermarket systems don't work as well as they could. Most of the systems try to relieve all the system back-pressure, when in fact at low rpm, back-pressure can help retain torque. Where you want reduced back pressure is during high rpm driving," said Hanson.

Hanson's observations are easy to understand when you look at many of the systems offered. Your factory exhaust system is not designed for maximum performance—that's a given. With over a dozen twists and turns, resonators, muffler restrictions, catalytic converter and tiny-diameter pipe, it doesn't take an Ed Hanson to see that the stock system has got to go. A simple muffler change will give you better engine response. Increasing the pipe diameter from the 1.75 inches to anything bigger also helps. Adding a massive tip does nothing to help performance—and in many cases looks ridiculous.

To achieve performance gains in Honda engines, it's the size of the exhaust tubing that is the critical factor. Some systems use giant 2.5- to 3-inch tubing to route gases to the muffler. "A three-inch tube on a Honda Civic is a waste of tubing. In fact, it can reduce performance over two-inch pipe," said Hanson. This is especially important for 1996 and newer Civics. The OBD systems in these models are extremely sensitive to changes and, when improperly disturbed, will affect horsepower in a negative way.

An exhaust system is designed to efficiently move gas out of the engine through a sound-denoting device (the muffler) and to deliver it to a safe place away from the passenger area. A performance exhaust system is designed to enhance engine response by moving a greater volume of exhaust with more velocity. The theory is very similar to that of air-intake systems. The difference in heat displacement is not a major issue, as it is in air intakes.

Exhaust tips can add a touch of flair to the system but should be selected to have a style related to the Civic, CRX or del Sol year and model. For example, on the del Sol the rear valance, roofline and taillights are all horizontal in shape, so a round tip would look out of place. On Civic sedans and

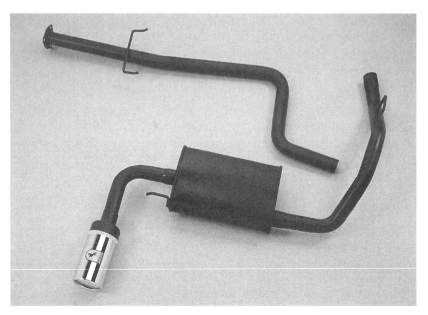

Fig. 4-9: Mate your new header to a performance exhaust system. There are many to choose from, all giving the sound of performance. Not all systems produce horsepower, so do your homework before selecting your system.

coupes a round tip fits better due to the curvature of the rear window frame.

Speaking of tips, there are only about 500 different items to choose from, ranging from round to oval to square and horizontal. It becomes an overload of shapes, sizes and finishes. You can choose from chrome, stainless, carbon fiber, powder coating, and billet aluminum; ones with baffles, doors, slots and grooves; single port, multi-exit, etc., etc. Over the past few years the popular trend is big, bigger and biggest, sometimes to the point where the tip is larger than the taillights. If you need to make a fashion statement, look to performance cars such as Ferrari, Corvette, Viper and Porsche for the lead. Don't weld a 10-inch tip on a 2.5-inch exhaust system just because everyone else is doing it. An ultra-large tip does nothing to help the car accelerate quicker or add to top-end performance.

The average aftermarket exhaust system will yield from five to seven horsepower. Most are designed to be installed using the factory attachment points with common tools. Install time can range from three to five hours.

In the case of custom-made exhaust systems, such as the ones built by Hanson, these can deliver as much as 15 additional horsepower. They are, however, not considered "bolt-on" because special fabrication, welding and fitting are necessary.

Power Ignition

One of the most misunderstood systems on any car is the ignition system. This is a complex combination of volts, amps, positive change, negative recharging, surge, coil-rise time, saturation time, milliseconds, nanoseconds—you get the idea.

Making sense of all this Einstein gibberish is enough to make even the most die-hard enthusiast throw up his hands in disgust. But it doesn't have to be this way. There are seven basic components that make your system work: alternator, distributor, coil, igni-

Fig. 4-10: Exhaust tip designs have gotten out of hand. It seems the logic is the bigger the better. Some tips offer a different approach, such as this shot gun tip. The door opens and closes with exhaust flow, helping to correct backpressure.

tion wires, spark plugs, ground strap and battery. Simply upgrading any one or all of these components can deliver more performance, but a breakdown of any one of them can steal power from the engine. And what's worse, this power loss is usually disguised as a more serious problem.

The first place to start with an ignition upgrade is the plugs and wires. Your Civic was likely originally equipped with platinum spark plugs, which are designed to last at least 50,000 miles. While these plugs offer years of trouble-free driving, they do so with little performance value. You sacrifice performance for longevity. Most common Civic owners are willing to compromise one to get the other. However, if you're reading this book, it's unlikely you're a common Civic owner.

Over the past decade an entirely new bounty of spark plugs has hit the market. Split-fork electrodes, fire circles, twin pulse firing, gold, silver, copper. How do you choose? Start with the metal used in the electrodes. It has already been established that platinum is a low carrier of energy. So, what's the highest carrier of energy? Of all the metals used to construct street-use spark plugs, silver has the greatest spark capacity. In years past, nearly every spark plug used copper as its base. Copper plugs are still the commodity spark plug and offer a good combination of spark power and longevity. Silver provides a greater spark but is compromised by a shorter life. Beru, manufacturers of the German-made Silverstone spark plug line, has only about 30,000 miles of life for its high-end performance plugs. With an average price of $6 per plug, this seems a bit expensive, but in a Civic that comes to only $24 for better performance. It is unlikely you'll find a more cost-effective way to increase horsepower.

Spark plugs come in a variety of heat settings. It is a common misunderstanding that a hotter plug will produce more power. The words "hot" and "cold" in reference to spark plugs can be confusing because a hot plug is used in a mild-built smog-controlled engine. A colder plug is used in a high-performance engine. The "hot" and "cold" terms refer to the spark plug's ability to transport heat from the firing end to the combustion chamber. A small SOHC Civic engine is an especially tough spark plug application because with mild upgrades (cam, timing gears, air intake) at idling, the engine needs a hotter plug. At higher rpm ranges a colder plug is better.

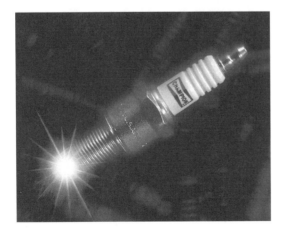

Fig. 4-11: There is so much hype surrounding spark plugs, it's easy to be confused. One thing is for sure: if you want performance, you have to start here. Getting rid of the low-energy platinum plugs is a beginning. From there, it's the jungle of forks, electrodes, casing, copper, gold, silver, multi-spark, etc., etc.

Plug tips have an optimum operating temperature of 700 degrees. When the plug tip gets any hotter, it often detonates prematurely, which can cause engine damage. A spark plug selection that is too hot will destroy itself and sometimes the engine within miles. This loss is accelerated when you run your Civic at heavy throttle.

At the other end of the spectrum, when the plugs are too cold (running around 350 degrees), unburned fuel creates carbon buildup. The first sign of this is loss of fuel economy. This is followed by after-ignition or run-on and then by loss of performance.

When you modify a Civic engine, even if it's just a simple intake and exhaust change, a spark plug change should be considered. Stock heat-range plugs can be replaced with slightly cooler plugs. If you have installed a supercharger or turbocharger or are using a nitrous oxide system, DO NOT USE EXTENDED-TIP SPARK PLUGS.

Spark power is generated not just by temperature ratings but equally in energy capacity. For this reason it can be more practical to keep a factory-recommended heat setting but to increase the energy capacity with a plug that offers a large-diameter electrode and improved insulator purity. Black aluminum oxide is commonly regarded as the racer's choice. Also, plugs that can deliver superior performance without the need of a suppressor or resistor can offer better energy flow.

Setting your plug gap is very important to maximizing engine efficiency. While many spark plug manufacturers pre-set the plug gap, it is a good idea to check each plug prior to installation. Also, if you are participating in a performance event (autocross or drag racing) bring an extra set of new plugs to the event. Before making your first run, install the new plugs. New plugs require as much as 18 percent less voltage to arc over. For everyday use, a used plug will make the gap wider by a process known as tip erosion, which requires the spark to jump from sharper areas off the electrode, stealing current and power.

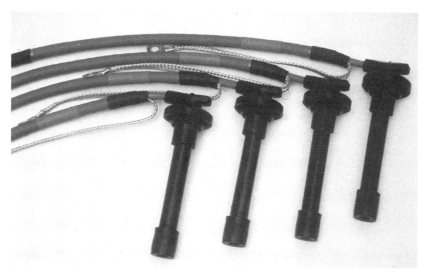

Fig. 4-12: Up until a few years ago nobody was pushing plug wires as a performance item. Today you have a wide range of choices. One company that has been a pioneer in the field is Nology. Nology wires feature a built-in capacitor to increase spark power by as much as 300 times over factory wires.

The greatest spark plugs in the world will yield nothing without a good set of performance wires. And there is no shortage of wild claims and theories about how and if wires work to improve horsepower. To understand how ignition wires work, think of the wires as a garden hose. The hose carries water from the faucet to the nozzle but can carry only a set volume of water, based on its diameter. A bigger hose can carry more water, provided there is enough water pressure to fill the hose. So it goes with ignition wires. Small-diameter wires, such as the factory-issued items, can transport only a small amount of spark energy from the coil to the distributor to the spark plugs. Increase the diameter and you increase the volume of energy you can deliver to the spark plugs.

Now that you have the basics, let's put a kink into the situation. Imagine you turn the water on and let it run freely out the open nozzle. While the water runs at a consistent flow, you soon discover that much of it is wasted. When you have the same water flow and fold or kink the line, pressure builds up. When released, the water surges with a quick and forceful burst. This is the way ignition wires work when a capacitor is inserted into the wire. The capacitor captures and holds the energy until the optimum time of ignition. When the volts are released it provides a powerful surge of energy.

During standard, pre-set factory operations of the average Civic (SOHC) engine, the crankshaft is required to rotate 135 degrees to complete the spark because the ignition wires need over three milliseconds in spark duration to complete combustion. With larger-diameter wires with greater current flow, this duration time can be decreased to about 100 degrees and one to two milliseconds of spark duration. With capacitor-equipped wires, the spark duration can be cut to as little as four nanoseconds (one million times shorter) using only about two degrees of crankshaft rotation.

To achieve power with a short spark life you need to increase the plasma arc. Larger wires, such as those from Magna Core and Vitek, supply more spark. Nology HotWires claim to increase spark energy by as much as 300 times over stock wires.

Ignition wires need to have vital elements to work effectively over a long period of time such as a good primary wire, proper heat insulation and quality boot material. Just because a wire looks fat doesn't mean it is a performance product. You should study the manufacturer's claims carefully before selecting ignition wires.

The next stop on the ignition journey is the coil. Bear in mind that late-model Civics come with internal activated coils. Factory-issued Honda coils work well for long-term, low-demand driving. After all, for 90 percent of Civic owners, day-to-day commuting is their purpose. For those owners the advantages of a high-performance coil means nothing. However, the performance-minded need a coil that offers a consistent level of power throughout the rpm range.

The coil is your power reserve. As in the flow-of-water analogy earlier in the chapter, the coil acts like a reservoir that stores the energy before it is needed. For performance functions, it is vital for the coil to deliver this energy in rapid succession. To achieve this, the coil must not only be powerful but must obtain quick rebound or "rise time." Ideally, you want over 30,000 volts of potential energy available at any given time. The factory coil can supply only about 25,000 volts and needs time to reload when drained. This is why under extreme conditions a hesitation or loss of power can occur with the stock coil. Aftermarket coils are available that can provide as much as 45,000 volts and have an ultra-fast rise time. This keeps the energy flowing from the coil to the distributor to the wires and onto the plugs.

If you pop the hood of your late-model Civic, you quickly come to the realization that the factory distributor cap has no attachment for an external coil; in fact, the coil is inside the distributor cap. For these, a special distributor cap is available that allows you to mount and use an aftermarket performance coil. This is the only recommended way to add a high-powered aftermarket coil to late-model Honda engines. Sure, you may have seen the factory cap drilled out and a homemade device adapted, but these are unreliable. When a superior aftermarket component is available, it is far better to choose that than to try to save a few bucks by creating something that may not work.

The final stop on the power flow trail is the alternator. For all the testing and trials

Dyno Testing Capacitor Equipped Ignition Wires
1996 Honda Civic EX SOHC

Acceleration

ACCELER. SPEED	BASELINE SECONDS	UPGRADED SECONDS
0-60	9.38	8.43
40-60	2.53	2.28
60-80	2.54	2.20
80-100	4.18	3.58

Adjusted Engine Output

RPM	BASELINE HP	UPGRADED HP
3,000	43	45
4,000	51	53
5,000	74	75
6,000	86	90
7,000	115	119
8,000	121	125

Power at the Wheels

RPM	BASELINE HP	UPGRADED HP
3,000	40	41
4,000	48	49
5,000	58	59
6,000	69	71
7,000	115	118
8,000	100	112

that performance geeks go through to find performance, most completely overlook the importance of the alternator. This is the component that generates the energy your ignition system needs. Often when an engine starts to falter, we look to find a major malfunction. For example, the engine begins to misfire or cough or is unresponsive at low rpm levels. It may idle rough or not at all. First, make sure all the plug wires are fully engaged. Next, remove the plugs and check for carbon build up or incorrect gap. Inspection of the wires should show no burns or cracks. The plugs look fine; the distributor cap is in good working order. Now what?

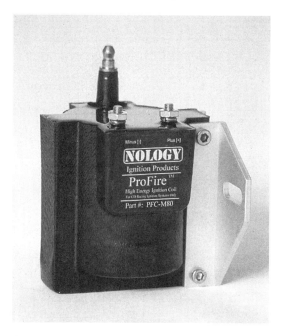

Fig. 4-13: For early-model Honda engines, installing an external coil is straightforward. As with everything these days, there are many to choose from. Look for a coil that supplies ample voltage and quick rise-time.

Fig. 4-14: A recent innovation is this aftermarket distributor cap, which allows you to install an external coil for late-model Civic engines. This replaces the factory cap, which houses an internal coil.

Before you start being a parts swapper, hoping to find the problem yourself, do a simple volt/ohm reading of your alternator. Often you will find this to be the problem.

Like the spark plugs, the Honda factory alternator works so well we just flat overlook the possibility it could be worn or defective. In older Civics and CRX models the alternator reading could be within acceptable range, but the wires and/or connectors weathered and no longer providing a solid contact point.

Or it could be that the increased, higher performance demands are overwhelming to the factory system. At any rate, more power is available. One trick is to install a more powerful alternator, such as one from Accel. Boosting the energy level of your alternator will give the performance coil more energy from which to draw. Audio components demand even more power from your alternator system. For the average Honda, a 50-amp alternator will handle the load needed to properly run your ignition system. For more overall power (when both performance

and massive audio is used) units can be found to supply as much as 140 amps.

Oh, yes, there is one more item to add to this story—the ground strap. Honda has one glaring weakness: the cheap ground strap that anchors the entire electrical system is a low-cost, near-useless piece of junk. However, this is the easiest item of all to upgrade. In a matter of five minutes you can replace the ground strap with a performance braided-steel selection from Nology. It's fast, inexpensive and better-looking, and it works.

ECU (On-Board Computers)

Finally, you're coming within sight of the end of the bolt-on battle. The final stop is the Civic computer control device, that magical box that hides your Honda's secrets. The scary mix of diodes, chips, circuits and black unknown components. This is it—the nerve center of your car. Do you dare dip into the forbidden pool of advanced technology?

Computer-controlled engines have evolved from simple fuel pressure monitoring systems into sophisticated brains that sense delicate changes in acceleration, valve timing, air density, fuel octane content, transmission function, speed-sensitive steering, braking—even your tires' air pressure. On-board computer controls have become a major part of Honda's engine components. Beginning with the need to automatically adjust fuel pressure flow to new fuel injection systems, a simple computer chip can keep the air/fuel density mixture consistent for a wide range of demands and conditions. The most obvious reason is that not everyone lives and drives cars at the same altitude. Mountain areas require adjustments different from those at sea level. This is why fuel injection controlled by computers is the standard of the industry, forever replacing the carburetor intake systems.

Like all manufacturers, Honda creates and programs its Civic, CRX and del Sol computer systems to provide smooth, trouble-free operation. Like all engine operations, your factory Civic was designed to fit the needs of common drivers. Being uncommon, you are aware you can quickly and safely reprogram your on-board ECU with a simple chip swap. In addition to adding horsepower, chips can also help you dial in increased fuel efficiency.

There are a number of companies that offer performance upgraded computer chips. To install these requires you to locate the ECU, pop open the factory seal, identify the operation chip, remove it and install the new chip. Sounds easy—a little too easy.

The one downfall of ECU chip changes is that they are not as simple as their counterparts from American and European automakers. Take BMW, for example. Once you remove and open the ECU, the chip swap is about as easy as adding RAM to your common Macintosh or IBM PC. Simply pop out the chip and install the new performance chip. The same ease of install holds true for GM cars.

However, in your Honda the chip is soldered into place, making the swap much more delicate to perform. The danger is if you damage any part of the ECU in the process, you're toast. Without the precise electronic equipment to find the damaged circuitry, it becomes hit or miss trial and error.

There are only a few well-chosen options for ECU upgrades. The preferred method is to *not* attempt to perform a chip or ECU change on your Honda in the comfort of your garage. The ECU upgrade is something best left to a facility that is equipped to do such work.

This is where the story can get scary. While these systems can be called "bolt-on," the price can be bank-busting. Furthermore, unless you're out to own a one-dimensional, drag-race-only, 10-second Civic, most of these systems are overkill. Take the Electromotive TEC-2 ECU, for example.

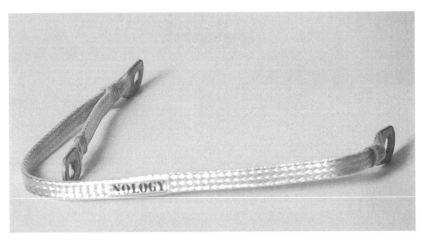

Fig. 4-15: Sometimes the smallest and simplest of items can make all the difference. The factory Honda ground strap robs the engine of electrical power. Immediately replace it with a braided steel ground strap and give your charging system a fighting chance.

Not only do you need to purchase the box, you also need the software package, a custom crank-angle sensor, dual-coil self-controlled ignition system and a pair of courtside tickets to the Knicks home games. This is hardcore stuff we're taking about here. Oh, one more thing: set aside about $1,200 for the right to play.

Want to get even more over the edge? Hook up the Motec ECU, the ultimate Honda tuner system. This bad boy can monitor nearly every engine function, handle traction control, provide data logging and advise what horse to pick at next year's Kentucky Derby. The Motec device is a marvel of electronics. Most die-hard Honda drag racers swear by them, even at $2,000 per unit.

But say, just for argument's sake, you are still going to drive your Civic on a day-to-day basis. For this you want a drivable upgrade that will get you to work and back and allow for a bit of tomfoolery on the weekend.

One of the most recommended units for real-world use is the Accel DFI. This black box handles the common functions, such as fuel pressures, rpm, ignition advance and retard, fuel curves and load-variance monitoring. And, because the Accel DFI is compatible with most Honda factory sensors, installation is less stressful.

The best method introduced to date for moderate performance improvements over a wide range of driving conditions is the Jet Performance program, which lets the manufacturer do all the work while you do all the tire-burning. It works like this: order the Jet Performance Computer Upgrade Package. When you open the box you'll be thinking it's a scam. The box is filled with a few forms and plenty of bubble wrap. This is where the fun begins. Fill out the information sheet, which asks for all the modifications you will ask your upgraded computer to work in harmony with—what air intake system, fuel deliver system, cam gears, exhaust, turbo or supercharger, nitrous, etc. Next, remove your ECU and wrap it in the bubble wrap. Send it (by next-day air) back to Jet Performance. The trained computer technicians at Jet then reprogram your ECU according to the information you have supplied. The ECU is packed and shipped back, ready to install.

Be aware of one very important point: a computer upgrade by itself will not yield the neck-snapping performance everyone claims. It's only one piece of the puzzle, not the entire picture. It is vital to always remember the most intelligent part of your Civic is you—the driver. You have ultimate control over how fast your car goes. Don't expect miracles from any one or even a combination of components. Oh—and one more thing: no matter what you do, how much you spend or what you claim, no one is ever the fastest. After 25 years of building and reporting on every type of car, from top fuel dragsters to go-carts, there is always somebody somewhere who's faster than you are. It's just the law of the asphalt jungle.

The most important thing to remember when it comes to bolt-on performance is to enjoy your car a little more tomorrow than you do today. That's the bottom line.

Fig. 4-16: This is the easiest way to juice up your on-board computer system. Pull the entire unit out and ship it off to one of the experts. These companies' products are well-designed to perform the upgrades.

Hard-Core Engine Performance

Fig. 5-1: Ten seconds to glory. If you want a street-and-strip blaster, the road is going to be a wild, bumpy, expensive ride—but worth the effort.

N ow you've gone and done it. After having a taste of bolt-on performance, you've got the uncontrollable urge to bite off large chunks of horsepower. You want speed and not just a little but a lot—and you want it now. Okay, sports fans, here we go. Get ready to dive into the deep end of the pool because this chapter is all about the hard-core stuff that 10-second dreams are made of.

Mind-numbing, vision-blurring performance begins here, with the internal engine components. Don't even think about mass-boost twin turbochargers and supercharging until you've earned the right of passage with the lowdown on pistons, rods, valve springs, cams, crankshafts, studs, angle-cut valves and all those go-fast, speed-demon parts you need to achieve screaming performance. A word of warning here: most hard-core performance-minded enthusiasts build a horsepower-rich engine to go drag racing. While this is fine, putting ultra-high performance on the street for everyday driving is not practical. Drivability of Civics with Superman status can be a pain in the racing seat, so if you have delusions of grandeur, take a few minutes to reflect on the day-to-day functions you ask of your little Honda. On the other hand, if it's a weekend warrior you want to be, then let's have at it.

Since there is no talking you out of this relentless quest to be master of Main Street, you will want to "stand" build your engine (that is, build it outside of the car) so you can still enjoy the use of your Civic until the killer engine is ready to install. This is the intelligent way to work, as it also allows you to keep the SOHC engine at the ready when and if you grenade your full-race, big-dog engine.

It's time to separate the haves from the have-nots. Supercharging, turbocharging, performance pistons, cams, cranks, rods, studs, engine swaps, nitrous and more. Wow, if you don't stop, you'll go blind.

Fig. 5-2: This is what we all would like to start with—the 1999 Honda Civic Si powerplant. If you're one of the lucky ones to have one, you're familiar with this appearance. All you need to do is add a turbo or supercharger and a little nitrous and you're good to go out and thump 5.0 Mustangs.

As in the chapter on bolt-ons, this portion of our quest is separated into basic component sections. However, before you go any further, first dispel the notion that you can push your SOHC 1.5 or 1.6L Civic engine to the promised land. It's not going to happen. For this chapter you're going to need a donor engine. The most popular is the 1.8L VTEC engine from an Acura Integra. These are in plentiful supply at your friendly local salvage yard. Speed tip: look for an Integra that has been smacked in the rear. Duh. The best engines have "B18B1" or "B18C1" stamped on the block. These are extremely strong engines to work with, and aftermarket speed parts are readily available. The other advantage is that the 1.8L is, for the most part, a bolt-in swap.

The next best choice, although a bit more pricey, is the 2.2L VTEC engine from a late-model Prelude. If you select this motor, you may find one a bit harder to come by: the demand for them is hot and heavy. Many auto salvage yards are hip to the import performance trend and start salivating when a totaled 'Lude is hooked on and coming through the front gate.

My choice is the 2.3 non-VTEC Prelude engine. The supply and price are better, and the bottom end of the engine can be built to supply superior torque, especially when you combine the bottom end with the 2.2L

VTEC head. Once you've determined which engines are available, you can start on your storybook journey.

Across the country there are a number of tuner shops specializing in building quick Honda engines. Most will simply ask you a few basic questions, such as:

1. How fast do you want to go?
2. How often do you want to rebuild?
3. How much money do you want to spend?

If money is no object you should seek out the best Honda engine minds on earth (such as John Concialdi at AEM or Oscar Jackson of Jackson Racing) and then take the first vital steps to becoming a local legend. If money is an object (and if you are starting with a Civic, it usually is), then you best keep reading to get the basic knowledge needed to get the job done. Be forewarned—this chapter is not going to show you step by step how to assemble the engine; it is going to focus on educating you on what to look for in the marketplace and how all this will relate to the Civic, CRX or del Sol you really want to drive.

It is important to remember that your donor engine will likely come from a common Honda or Acura. While Honda builds one of the finest engines in the industry, the inter-

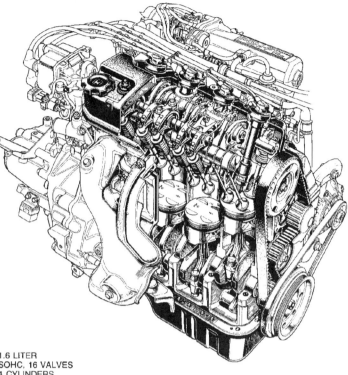

Fig. 5-3: Here's what most of us are destined to start with. The tried and true 1.6L SOHC engine is a fine work-horse for the street. With internal and bolt-on changes it can get into the 200 horsepower range.

1.6 LITER
SOHC, 16 VALVES
4 CYLINDERS
DISPLACEMENT: 1590cc
MULTI-POINT PROGRAMMED FUEL INJECTION
MAXIMUM HP: 105 @ 6000 RPM
MAXIMUM TORQUE: 98 LB-FT @ 5000 RPM

Fig. 5-4: Pulling the 1.8L engine from an Integra and transplanting it into a Civic is nearly a bolt-in proposition. As seen here, the engine compartment of an Integra configuration is similar to late-model Civics.

nal components are not engineered to handle superchargers, turbochargers or nitrous oxide systems. During the course of your quest you will be replacing pistons, cams, rings, rods, studs and perhaps even the crank.

When a "10-second drag race" Civic is spoken about, few enthusiasts realize what it takes to achieve such results. Racing is not only about creating horsepower. Results are about power-to-weight and the ability to control or put that power to the pavement.

First off, you need to know the math (and you thought your high school classes were going to be a waste). One horsepower equals the ability to do work equal to that of lifting 33,000 pounds one foot in one minute. (This is widely accepted to be the capability of an average horse.) Dr. Watts, who introduced the steam engine, developed this formula in an effort to sell the remarkable usable function of his steam engine. He rounded the answer to 33,000 pounds-feet per minute (or 550 pounds-feet per second). This became the average measurement for 1.0 horsepower.

It has been proven that to bring a 3,000-pound rear-wheel drive car down a quarter mile in less than 13 seconds requires a speed of 134 miles per hour. Therefore, 275 horsepower is needed to push a stripped-down Camaro or Mustang through the traps in 12.99 seconds. To break the 10-second territory, a massive 600 horsepower would be needed.

Oscar Jackson, the recognized professor of Honda power, estimated front-wheel drive driveline loss of 14 percent is common for GS-R transmissions with stock tires. Therefore, over 500 horsepower is required to bring a 2,000 pound CRX or Civic into the same neighborhood. Your average street-driven Civic weighs in at 2,800 pounds (wet, with driver). Therefore, for a Civic with a SOHC engine and factory transmission with Plus One tire and wheel upgrade, you would need to generate 680 horsepower to record a 9.87-second ET. You can quickly see why the factory 1.6L SOHC Honda engine is an unlikely candidate for a 10-second record breaker.

Here's a quick reference chart to determine horsepower to weight and 1/4 mile ET.

Now that you are fully convinced the SOHC engine is overmatched for the horsepower needed to make serious 1/4-mile impressions, it is time to get to work on that 1.8L VTEC, 2.2L VTEC or 2.3L Prelude powerplant. Most engine swaps into Civic or CRX models are straightforward and can be completed with only a few minor modifications to the engine and transmission mounts. When you acquire the engine, get the tranny and transaxle as a complete unit, because the Civic transaxle is not adequate to handle the power you are going to achieve. The Acura GS-R or any VTEC transaxle has the capability to be beefed up to accommodate the added torque. The GS-R is the preferred choice because of its wheel-to-wheel measurement (it is closer to the same track as the Civic).

Horsepower and Weight = 1/4 Mile ET

WEIGHT	HORSEPOWER								
	240	275	300	330	360	390	425	450	480
2000	12.55	12.07	11.65	11.30	10.95	10.65	10.55	10.30	10.10
2200	12.95	12.45	12.03	11.65	11.32	11.02	10.75	10.50	10.25
2400	13.30	12.80	12.38	12.00	11.70	11.35	11.00	10.78	10.50
2600	13.75	13.20	12.75	12.34	12.00	11.76	11.38	11.15	10.90
2800	14.06	13.60	13.07	12.70	12.30	12.00	11.70	11.40	11.10
3000	14.40	13.85	13.36	12.96	12.55	12.25	11.99	11.70	11.40
3200	14.70	14.12	13.66	13.23	12.85	12.50	12.15	11.93	11.64

Honda Engine Swap Information

Engine Code	Size	Cam	HP Rating	Induction
EW1	1.5L	SOHC	76	**Carburetor**

Where to Find It: 1984–87 CRX, Civic; 1984–85 Civic S.

Comments: Very few parts available. Not recommended for performance use. A good basic throwaway engine.

Installation Difficulty: Bolts into 1984–90 Civics and CRXs.

Engine Code	Size	Cam	HP Rating	Induction
EW3	1.5L	SOHC	91	**MPI**

Where to Find It: 1985–87 CRX Si, Civic; 1986–87 Civic Si.

Comments: Some parts are available but are hard to find and will only supply moderate power. Effort and money are better spent on a more contemporary engine block.

Installation Difficulty: Bolts into 1984–90 Civics and CRXs.

Engine Code	Size	Cam	HP Rating	Induction
D15A	1.5L	SOHC	93	**MPI**

Where to Find It: 1986–87 CRX, Civic; 1987 Civic S.

Comments: Expect only mild power gains.

Installation Difficulty: Bolts into 1986–90 Civics and CRXs.

Engine Code	Size	Cam	HP Rating	Induction
D15B6	1.5L	SOHC	70	**TBI**

Where to Find It: 1988–91 CRX and Civic HF.

Comments: Limited parts offerings. Only mild power gains.

Installation Difficulty: Bolts into 1984–98 Civics.

Fig. 5-5: Paul Rosenthal was one of the first Honda guys to make major horsepower from a street-based Civic. This 1.6L pumped out 200 horsepower. He debuted this purple coupe in 1991.

Fig. 5-6: One of the most plentiful and logical engine swaps is the Integra 1.8L DOHC powerplant. Starting with 140 horsepower, this engine is found in 1992-97 Integra RS and LS models. It is a fairly straightforward swap.

Honda Engine Swap Information *continued*

Engine Code	Size	Cam	HP Rating	Induction
D16A6	1.6L	SOHC	110	MPI

Where to Find It: 1988–91 CRX Si and Civic Si.

Comments: Excellent parts availability, including low-, medium- and high-compression pistons.

Installation Difficulty: Bolts into 1986–98 Civics.

D16Z6	1.6L	SOHC (VTEC)	125	MPI

Where to Find It: 1992–95 Civic EX, Civic Si; 1993–95 del Sol Si.

Comments: The best of all SOHC engines. Plenty of internal parts available. Can be built to deliver over 250 horsepower (without nitrous oxide).

Installation Difficulty: Bolts into all post-84 Civics.

D16Z7	1.6L	SOHC (VTEC)	127	MPI

Where to Find It: 1996–00 Civic EX

Comments: Uses many of the same components as D16Y7 engine. VTEC feature makes engine more desirable and versatile.

Installation Difficulty: Bolts into 1990–00 Civics.

B18A1	1.8L	DOHC	140	TPI

Where to Find It: 1990–97 Acura Integra LS, RS and GS

Comments: Perhaps the most popular engine to swap over into Civic, CRX and early del Sol models. Good selection of parts available with excellent power potential.

Installation Difficulty: Bolts into 1988–99 Civics. Air intake clearance problems on CRX and del Sol.

B16A1	1.6L	DOHC	130-160	MPI

Where to Find It: 1990–91 CRX Si, Civic Si-R (Japan); 1992–95 Civic Si-R (Japan); 1993–95 del Sol (VTEC); 1986–89 Acura Integra LS and GS.

Comments: Most go-fast parts available but from limited suppliers. Also known as ZCG.

Installation Difficulty: Bolts into 1990–98 Civics.

B18C	1.8L	DOHC (VTEC)	190	MPI

Where to find it: 1997–00 Acura Integra Type-R

Comments: An excellent engine set-up. Engine only available in Japanese models. Careful not to confuse this with the B18C1.

Installation difficulty: Bolts into 1993–00 Civics.

Honda Engine Swap Information *continued*

Engine Code	Size	Cam	HP Rating	Induction
B17A1	1.7L	DOHC (VTEC)	160	MPI

Where to find it: 1992–93 Acura Integra GS-R.

Comments: A very good upper and lower engine combination from the 1993 Integra GS-R. Although a rare engine it shares many of the same engine components as the B18C1.

Installation difficulty: Bolts into 1990–99 Civics.

B18C1	1.8L	DOHC (VTEC)	170	MPI

Where to find it: 1994–97 Acura Integra GS-R.

Comments: This is the bomb. Perhaps the best of all VTEC engines produced. Every part is available to build a 10-second street rocket. Can be found on 1994–98 Integra GS-R models.

Installation difficulty: Bolts into 1990–99 Civics. Will require fabrication for limited-slip transaxle.

A20A3	2.0L	SOHC	110	MPI

Where to find it: 1987–89 Accord; 1985–87 Prelude.

Comments: Don't bother wasting your time.

Installation difficulty: Bolts into most Civics with fabricated engine mounts. Clearance problems for exhaust header.

F22A4	2.2L	SOHC	140	MPI

Where to find it: 1990–97 Accord; 1992–96 Prelude.

Comments: Good availability of parts. Moderate power gains.

Installation difficulty: Difficult engine swap. Requires fabricated engine and transaxle mounts. Clearance problems with exhaust and induction linkage.

C27A4	2.7	DOHC V6	170	MPI

Where to find it: 1986–90 Acura Legend; 1995–97 Accord LX and EX.

Comments: Not worth the extreme effort to make the swap. Limited supply of performance parts.

Installation difficulty: Very difficult engine swap. Requires fabricated engine and transaxle mounts. Clearance problems with exhaust header and induction linkage as well as extreme difficulty in performing common maintenance.

F23A1	2.3	SOHC (VTEC)	150	MPI

Where to find it: 1996–99 Acura CL, 1998–00 Accord.

Comments: Few parts available. Modest gains at best.

Installation difficulty: Difficult engine swap. Requires fabricated engine and transaxle mounts. Clearance problems with exhaust header and induction linkage.

Honda Engine Swap Information *continued*

Engine Code	Size	Cam	HP Rating	Induction
J30A1	3.0L	SOHC (VTEC) V6	200	MPI

J30A1

Where to find it: 1998–00 Accord LX and EX, 1996–99 Acura CL.

Comments: Engine can get good horsepower gains. Parts selection is growing.

Installation difficulty: Very difficult engine swap. Requires fabricated engine and transmission mounts. Clearance problems with exhaust headers. May require setting the engine back into the firewall. For drag racing, a narrowed Ford nine-inch rear end could be used. For street or road racing use, transplant the independent rear suspension from the NSX or Acura Vigor.

Engine Code	Size	Cam	HP Rating	Induction
F23A5	2.2L	SOHC	120	MPI

F23A5

Where to find it: 1991–94 Accord

Comments: Bad choice—few parts are available and only small performance gains can be realized.

Installation difficulty: Difficult engine swap. Requires fabricated engine and transaxle mounts. Clearance problems with exhaust header and induction linkage.

Engine Code	Size	Cam	HP Rating	Induction
B20A5	2.0L	SOHC	140	MPI

B20A5

Where to find it: 1988-90 Prelude, 1991 Prelude Si.

Comments: Very few parts available.

Installation difficulty: Moderate engine swap. Requires fabricated engine and transaxle mounts.

Fig. 5-7: If money is no object or barrier, this is the new hot ticket in import performance racing. The 3.0L NSX engine can be built to deliver over 600 horsepower. However, for Civics, CRXs and especially del Sols, this requires major fabrication and engineering. For drag racing, install a narrowed nine-inch Ford rear end. For road racing, the rear suspension of the NSX works quite well.

Fig. 5-8: This is a 2.2L VTEC engine as seen in a 1997 Prelude. The engine will take up more space in your Civic, which will cause clearance problems for the exhaust header and throttle linkage. It may also make adding a long-pipe cold-air intake more difficult. However, the horsepower output can be incredibly rewarding.

Honda Engine Swap Information *continued*

Engine Code	Size	Cam	HP Rating	Induction
F22A1	**2.2L**	**SOHC**	**145**	**MPI**

F22A1

Where to find it: 1990–97 Accord, 1992–96 Prelude S.

Comments: Good low cost engine. Very strong bottom end. Some parts available.

Installation difficulty: Difficult engine swap. Requires fabricated engine and transaxle mounts. Clearance problems with exhaust header and induction linkage.

C30A1	**3.0L**	**SOHC (VTEC) V6**	**280**	**MPI**

C30A1

Where to find it: 1991–00 Acura NSX.

Comments: Engine now a favorite for extensive horsepower gains. Parts selection is growing as NSX racing getting more popular.

Installation Difficulty: Very difficult engine swap. Requires fabricated engine and transmission mounts. Clearance problems with exhaust headers. May require setting the engine back into the firewall. For drag racing, a narrowed Ford nine-inch rear end could be used. For street or road racing use, transplant the independent rear suspension from the NSX or Acura Vigor.

H23A1	**2.3L**	**DOHC**	**150**	**MPI**

H23A1

Where to find it: 1998–99 Accord, 1996–99 Acura CL

Comments: Excellent choice. Especially strong bottom end. Many parts available.

Installation difficulty: Difficult engine swap. Requires fabricated engine and transaxle mounts. Clearance problems with exhaust header and induction linkage.

H22A1	**2.2L**	**DOHC (VTEC)**	**195**	**MPI**

H22A1

Where to find it: 1992–96 Prelude VTEC, 1997–99 Prelude Si, 1997 Prelude SH.

Comments: The ultimate engine swap choice. Everything is available to make major horsepower.

Installation difficulty: Moderate engine swap. May require fabricated engine and transaxle mounts in most Civics. Clearance problems with exhaust header and throttle linkage.

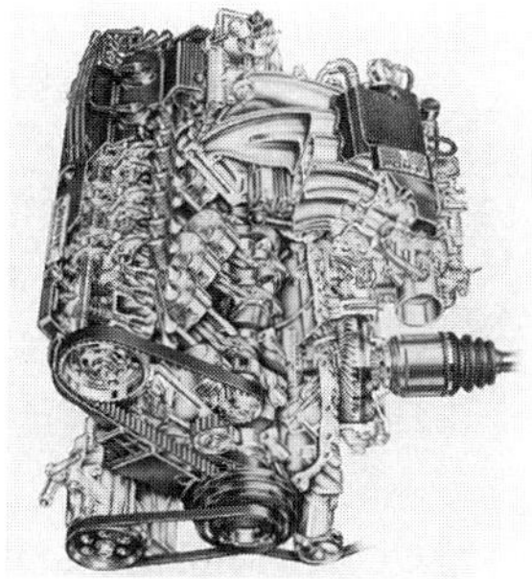

Fig. 5-9: If sanity is no concern, try the most difficult install of them all. Yank out the 1.6L Civic engine and drop in the 2.5L inline five-cylinder engine from the ill-fated Acura Vigor. The engine supplies 176-horsepower and remarkable torque. In the Vigor, the engine was mounted longitudinally, helping to achieve a near-ideal 60/40 front/rear weight distribution, perfect for FWD configuration.

Once again, engine selection is vital. For a B18 engine or VTEC "C," the engine is blessed with a more than suitable crank and girdled main caps. These features, by contrast, are found only on full-race American V8 engines, making either one of these engine blocks nearly failure-free. The only procedures you need to perform on the crank are to knife-edge the counterweights and dynamically balance the reworked unit. This trick lightens the rotating mass, which in turn allows for the engine to rev higher and provide better throttle response.

Next, replace the head bolts with studs. Studs can be more accurately torqued than bolts and provide greater integrity and reduce the stress points commonly caused by bolts. Remember, you're going to ask the cylinders to handle an extreme amount of pressure. Look for head studs made from 8740 Chrome Moly Steel. This material holds up very well under demanding conditions.

While you've got the engine apart and nicely secured on your engine stand (don't be cheap—before you start your engine swap, buy an engine assembly stand), you should replace the bearing. A good overall choice is one with multithicknesses, which allow for greater clearance from the Honda bearings. This clearance provides improved oil flow and keeps the bearings cooler under the extreme demands of high rpm operation.

Oil cavitation is something we'll be talking about when it comes to lubricants and chemicals. However, this is an important term when you modify your oil pump. The two lifebloods of your engine are oil and water. And while the two should never meet, your engine can't run without them. Honda blessed us all with one of the best factory oil pumps available. Even at high-speed levels exceeding 10,000 rpm, the factory oil pump works with remarkable precision and durability. About the only logical step to perform is to shim the

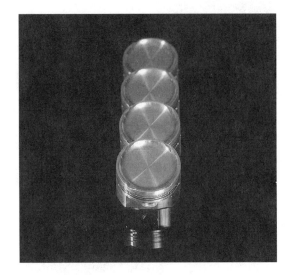

Fig. 5-10: The first stop on the horsepower trip is pistons. There are different options as to which composition offers the most power with leader-edge durability. These AEM dish Honda pistons are engineered using the same techniques used by Honda Formula One teams. The trick is to determine the final induction process. Turbo and supercharging will require different, often lower-compression-ratio pistons than normally aspirated engines.

relief spring. This may deliver about 10 extra psi (pounds per square inch) of oil pressure. There has been a lot of talk about radiusing the inlet and outlet ports to reduce oil cavitation forming. Although this is a nice to have, it is not necessary.

Now that you've got the block prepared, you have to choose pistons and rods. When researching pistons, the most common term you'll hear is "compression ratio." After a dozen years of hanging around Honda performance geeks, I can say that nearly 90 percent of them have little or no clue what and how compression ratios work or how they play a part in high-performance engine-building. Most people believe that the higher the compression ratio, the tricker the engine must be. To help put you into the top 10 percent of your class, here's the formula for determining the compression ratio of an engine:

$$\frac{\text{Cylinder head volume} + \text{Swept volume of cylinder} + \text{Head gasket volume} + \text{Piston volume}^*}{\text{Cylinder head volume} + \text{Head gasket volume} + \text{Piston volume}^*}$$

*This could be positive or negative, depending on if the piston is a dish or dome head.

Here's a simple example:

The cylinder head volume is 45cc's. The swept volume of the cylinder is 400cc's. Head gasket volume equals 6cc's. Piston dish and valve notches are 5cc's. Therefore:

$$\frac{45 + 400 + 6 + 5}{45 + 6 + 5}$$

The above formula equals a compression ratio of 8.14:1.

Right about now you've got to be scratching your head in total bewilderment. How on earth do you figure out swept volume? Take the bore times two to the second power, times stroke—this equals swept volume. This is critical because small changes in bore diameter can make significant differences in compression ratios. For example, 81mm bore 90 stroke (8.5) to the second power × 3.142 × 90)/1000 = 463.77cc/cylinder. If the conversion of mm to the third power to cc to the third power is confusing (that's an understatement), simply divide by 1000 at the end of the equation, then convert the bore and stroke to cm instead of mm (or divide by 10).

Even if you're totally confused about how all this works, just feel relieved that experts at JG Engine Dynamics, AEM, Crower Cams and Arias Pistons have done all the math for you. However, if you can commit these formulas to memory, you'll be pretty impressive at your next car club meeting.

High-performance pistons generally come in three compression ratios: low-compression pistons (8.5:1) for moderate-to-high-boost supercharged and turbocharged engines; O.E.-compression pistons for power replacement and engines with moderate horsepower and/or nitrous oxide; and high-compression pistons (12.5:1) for ultra-high-performance engines without superchargers or high-boost turbochargers. There are many manufacturers who offer high-performance pistons. The key features to look for are the material from which they are made, how

complete the set is and the recommended ratio for the fuel induction system you will be installing.

There are counterbalanced theories about piston material content. For example, JG Engine Dynamics has a zero content of silicon. JG claims that a lack of silicon makes pistons stronger and less likely to crack. AEM pistons are specially engineered, incorporating the same tolerances used in engines for Honda's Formula One race cars. These pistons are made from 4032 high silicon. Just like in any raging debate, you will need to examine each carefully before making the decision on which to use. Whichever piston brand you select, the pistons should include rings and wrist pins and full instructions for setting ring gap, bore finishing and final block preparation.

Speaking of block preparation, all the experts agree you should sleeve (some refer to sleeves as liners) your cylinders prior to installing high-performance pistons. There are two basic sleeves—those with a thin wall for stock rebuilding and those with a thicker wall for blocks that have been over-bored.

Okay, you still have a few bucks left in the bank. Get ready to drain the checking account or go without drive-through burgers for the next two months. Porting and polishing the head provides the kind of flow needed to achieve major league horsepower. However, headwork is not cheap. In addition to the shop work, you're going to need lightweight valves that are angle-cut to maximize flow. If you're smart, you'll be replacing the stock valve springs and retainers as well. Nothing is more frustrating than having a potentially good run ruined by a snapped valve spring. Perhaps the best kept secret in valve springs are the ones offered by Eibach. That's right—Eibach, the suspension company. Eibach has been supplying valve springs to Formula One engine builders for years. However, recently these ultra-high-quality applications have become available for street-based engines as well. For the vast

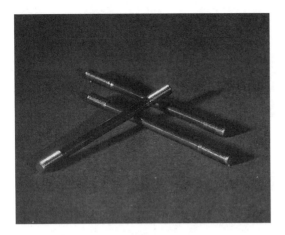

Fig. 5-11: Aftermarket head studs are one of the easiest items to install. Getting rid of the head bolts in favor of head studs allows you to torque down the head with more precise levels.

majority of engine builders, DPR valve springs and titanium retainers have been the product of choice.

With the head at the machine shop and the pistons on your workbench, you need connecting rods. High-performance connecting rods are to durability what pistons are to power. It is critical that connecting rods be as strong as possible, yet light-weight. These are precision components and must be capable of exceeding red-line revolutions for sustained periods of time. After tests of Crower rods and Hyper Rods from AEM, both passed the performance grade. Tests were conducted on engines used in both road racing and drag racing as well during dyno testing. Both AEM and Crower rods passed with no measurable wear factors.

Selecting camshafts will be the second most difficult task you will face while building your engine. The most difficult task?—defending your choice of the camshafts.

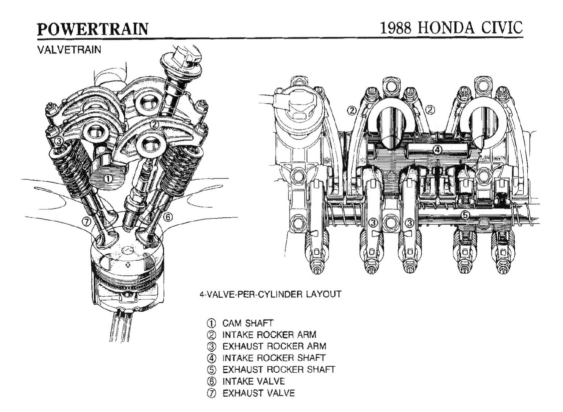

POWERTRAIN   1988 HONDA CIVIC
VALVETRAIN

4-VALVE-PER-CYLINDER LAYOUT

① CAM SHAFT
② INTAKE ROCKER ARM
③ EXHAUST ROCKER ARM
④ INTAKE ROCKER SHAFT
⑤ EXHAUST ROCKER SHAFT
⑥ INTAKE VALVE
⑦ EXHAUST VALVE

Fig. 5-12: Head and valve work, even on SOHC engines, is not a cheap proposition. This cutaway illustration details the inner workings of a Civic's valvetrain. Try to imagine the cam spinning at 7,000 rpm. Now you get an idea of why precision-cut valves and high-performance valve springs are so important.

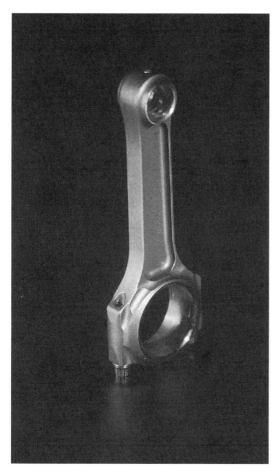

Fig. 5-13: You're going to need something strong and precise to attach power pistons to. Performance rods are vital to keeping horsepower reliable and durable. Don't hack your budget by using the O.E. rods. Spending a few extra bucks on the right rods is better than ripping open the engine after you bend or break a stock rod.

First, you should know that all aftermarket camshafts begin life as stock Honda cams. In other words, there are no aftermarket manufacturers of Honda performance camshafts. Every engine-builder has his own favorite grind. Some select mild and others choose radical; still others do nothing to the original cams. Ironically, all three selections have been used as part of the 10-second puzzle. As you will notice the surge of power over the 4,000-rpm mark, you will also be painfully aware of the rough idle and lack of smooth operation at low rpm levels. What high-lift, long-duration cams give you is that snap-like throttle response

as the valves open and close in performance time, eliminating valve lag.

What most top engine-builders agree on is that to get super-high rev action (9,000-10,000 rpm) special grind cams are necessary. However, if your aim is to mix street, strip and sport activities, the factory cams (especially on VTEC engines) will serve you very well.

Now here you are with all the engine components ready to assemble. You've busted the bank and would have taken out a second trust on the family home if you thought for a minute you could have gotten away with it. With great care you are about to select the bolt-on items (see Chapter 4) to make all those internal engine items worth the money. Hopefully you will never have to see the pistons, rods, sleeves, valves, valves springs and crank ever again, but don't count on it. But before you drive in the pistons, drop in the cams and torque down the studs, I've got a few juicy tricks for you.

There is a little invention released a short time ago that is a smart and cost-effective way to help maintain engine integrity. It is called Block Guard. This is a precision-formed aluminum brace that converts an open-deck engine block into a solid unit, which instantly adds strength and durability to selected Honda engine applications. This is a drop-on product—no machining is needed. What Block Guard does is to help prevent movement during compression stokes, which can cause head gasket failure. This is a $200 insurance policy well worth the coin, especially after you have forked out a few grand to complete the performance engine upgrade.

What about that other trick? How about adding a little O.E. domestic item to your Honda? Many quick Hondas run a secret weapon—a Ford throttle body unit. Just find yourself a Ford Mustang and transplant the 65mm throttle body unit. This may, depending on your engine, require a small amount of fabrication. However, your go-fast engine is going to need the extra airflow.

What? You want more power? You're an animal and nothing is going to stand in the way of your being the ultimate boulevard marauder, not even selling all your worldly possessions. Okay, Hotshot, let's talk superchargers, turbochargers and nitrous oxide.

Starting with superchargers and turbochargers: these two devices are the primary weapons of mass combustion. While both can deliver large amounts of horsepower gain, they work on different theories. In small, high-revving engines, some power brokers like a supercharger because it substantially improves low-end torque. This is especially important on 1.6L and 1.8L engines. Turbochargers, on the other hand, work very well in larger Honda engines and in the higher rpm range, providing a surge of power under acceleration.

Some Japanese cars work better with one or the other. For example, Toyota's MR2 first offered a supercharged model, then switched to a turbocharger. The turbocharged MR2 was a superior performer. Other cars, like the Mazda Miata, find favor in either choice. A roots-based supercharger gives a Miata the low-end torque the engine needs. A turbocharger allows the high-revving engine with the boost needed to blow past 5.0 Mustangs. Like the Miata, most 1.6L and 1.8L Hondas can successfully go either way. For 2.0, 2.2 and 2.3L Honda engines, turbochargers have recorded a high success rate. First, you need to have a basic understanding of how both superchargers and turbochargers create power.

Turbochargers

Before you get all hot and bothered in anticipation of discovering the secrets of turbos, you should understand that this section is giving only the basics. If you want to know everything about turbocharging, order a copy of *Maximum Boost* by Corky Bell, who is the absolute expert on turbochargers and how to get the most from them.

As Bell points out in his book, nearly one-third of your engine's potential energy is lost out of the tailpipe in the form of heat. This means if you can get 200 horsepower from your engine, you're letting a possible 70 bhp escape into the ozone. A turbocharger helps you recover this energy and turn it into extra horsepower.

Exhaust gases drive a turbocharger. The flow of exhaust pushes the turbines inside the housing, creating mass airflow. This increase in airflow can be turned into power. (Remember that air velocity is more important than air volume.) However, because hot exhaust gases move the turbo and an air pump is a heat-creating device, the best you can hope for is an efficiency rating of about 60 percent. Unless, of course, you install an intercooler to lower the air temperature before it reaches the intake system. When you intercool the incoming air, the boost factor can be increased, and thus more power can be made.

Like any form of horsepower gain, turbocharging is driven by more than exhaust gases—it is driven by money. The more money you lay on the counter, the greater

Fig. 5-14: Until space invaders take over the Earth, the debate will rage over what's better—turbochargers or superchargers. While this Turbonetics unit is the basis on which a good power induction system starts, an intercooler is often needed to bring the air temperature down to a potent level. For street use, at higher rpm, a turbocharger turns a mild pretender into a true contender.

your potential power gain. For example, the basic turbocharger package includes the turbo unit, boost control, plumbing, exhaust manifold, hoses, brackets, etc. Cost: about $2,000. If you want an intercooler, tack on another 300-500 bucks. Want more power? Order a bigger turbo and a larger intercooler. Don't forget an oil cooler and larger fuel injectors. By the time all is said and done, you've got 4Gs into your turbo kit.

Superchargers

Unlike turbochargers, superchargers do not require the use of exhaust gases to drive them. A supercharger works off a belt, much like any other accessory connected to your engine. This is the main reason superchargers have a lower efficiency rating than turbochargers. However, it is also the reason the power is more responsive on the low end of the power band.

A supercharger's true worth is measured not by bulk power gain but by net gain. To get this number you must take the bulk power gain and subtract the energy it takes to drive the device. Generally the supercharger (many old school performance buffs still refer to it as a "blower") runs off the

Fig. 5-15: One of the advantages of turbos is the upgrades you can make. This cross-section of the Turbonetics Ball-Bearing unit shows one of the hottest items on the turbocharging frontier.

same belt as the power steering, smog pump and alternator. The crank drives this via the lower pulley. Like the turbocharger, a supercharger spins at tremendous speed, rapidly increasing the velocity of the air forced into the induction system. Also like a turbocharger, the supercharger is, for all practical purposes, an air pump—and we have already determined that an air pump operating at high speed creates heat, the perfor-

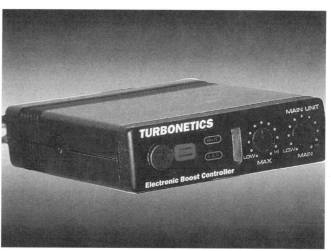

Fig. 5-16: A true turbocharging system requires many components. Ultra-high-performance wastegate and turbo timer or boost controls are necessary items to maximize turbo power.

mance freak's enemy. However, according to Honda performance expert Oscar Jackson, the intake degrees of a root-based supercharger is much lower and does not require an intercooler.

Superchargers can supply as much as a 40 percent increase in power and do it with a lower boost factor—in many cases as low as 6 psi. This is why many high-performance experts praise the reliability of superchargers for street car use. Oscar Jackson has experimented with both turbo and superchargers in all types of Honda and Acura engines, as well as in Mazda Miatas. After years of tuning, he is convinced that a root-based supercharger is far more usable on the street than any turbocharger kit.

As for cost and ease of installation, superchargers win over turbos on both counts. A complete supercharger package for a 1.6L Honda engine runs about $2,700 and will add around 40 horsepower. This is without making any other engine changes—internal or bolt-on.

Where superchargers lose to turbochargers is in upgrades. Once the supercharger is in place, you can only increase the boost factor and add an intercooler. Turbo systems are available in small to ridiculous, with intercoolers to match. Plus, you can upgrade from single to dual turbochargers.

So what's the bottom line? For my money—and I would spend mine like I would yours—I like the supercharger route. That's because I would never build a car I couldn't drive on a daily basis. Superchargers provide a better working torque range for low and high rpm driving without the lag inherent in turbochargers. Oh—and I like the cost, appearance and sound of the supercharger as well.

Nitrous Oxide

If horsepower were a fruit, nitrous oxide would be the juice. This is the great equalizer, the little shot of super-cold gas that

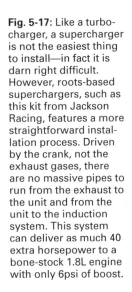

Fig. 5-17: Like a turbocharger, a supercharger is not the easiest thing to install—in fact it is darn right difficult. However, roots-based superchargers, such as this kit from Jackson Racing, features a more straightforward installation process. Driven by the crank, not the exhaust gases, there are no massive pipes to run from the exhaust to the unit and from the unit to the induction system. This system can deliver as much 40 extra horsepower to a bone-stock 1.8L engine with only 6psi of boost.

exploits power like nothing else can. Nitrous is the lowest-cost, most convenient method to develop instant acceleration.

Nitrous oxide increases power through two basic chemical/physical principles. To understand this let us travel back to high school once again, this time to the chemistry lab. Nitrous oxide is composed of nitrogen and oxygen. When these two gases are combined, the blend becomes 150 times more oxygen-rich than air. Stored as a liquid at 900 psi, nitrous oxide flashes to vapor when dropped to atmospheric pressure (as it is sprayed into an engine). When this flash takes place it becomes super-cool, often to as much as –37 degrees. This super-cold charge of nitrous and gas entering the combustion chamber is so dense and compacted, when ignited by the spark plug, the burn is massive and extremely powerful. This pushes the pistons down with more force than the common air/gasoline mixture.

According to Dr. Christopher Jacobs, a respected expert on automotive electronics who travels the country lecturing on the attributes of engine performance, "All other conditions being equal, the hotter and more rapidly the gasoline burns, the more horsepower the engine generates. When both of these effects work simultaneously, nitrous oxide can easily double engine horsepower at a press of a button."

"The quick, hot-burn condition is one reason why ultra-high-performance ignition wires are so important when using nitrous," said Nology's Werner Funk. But be forewarned that high-grade ignition wires are only the start of the entire nitrous oxide precautions. Because nitrous systems are so easy to install, most first-time users simply remove the fuel injection system, install a fogger plate at the entrance to the manifold, run the lines, valve and switch and secure the bottle. When a shot of nitrous is injected, a massive power surge is experienced. So with the next run the shot is longer and the results are more dramatic. On the third run the button is pressed a bit longer and the sound heard is the engine blowing apart.

Installing a nitrous system means hooking up a *complete* system, including safety controls, such as a control panel to monitor the amount of nitrous to gas. When installed properly, this type of control will shut down the nitrous when the mixture becomes too dense, thus saving your engine from certain disaster.

Experienced racers use a rapid shot of nitrous for racing to quickly spool up an oversized turbocharger. This is powerful stuff, to

Fig. 5-18: If you need an extra shot of power (and who doesn't?), try a little nitrous oxide. A simple press of a button can deliver 50-150 horsepower. Just use it with caution—a good engine is a terrible thing to waste.

WHO OFFERS WHAT

PISTONS	RODS	STUDS
AEM	AEM	AEM
Arias	Carrillo	ARP
JE Pistons	Crower	
JG Engine Dynamics	Cunningham	
JUN	JUN	
ProPower	Spoon Sports	
Spoon Sports		

CAMS	CRANKS	VALVE SPRINGS
Bullfrog	JUN	Eibach
Crane	Spoon Sports	DPR
JUN		JUN
JG Engine Dynamics		
Skunkworks		
Spoon Sports		
ZAK Motorsports		

THROTTLE BODY UNITS	VALVES
BBK	DPR
JG Engine Dynamics	JG Engine Dynamics

TURBOCHARGERS	SUPERCHARGERS	NITROUS
AXZ	Endyn	NOS
Alamo Motorsports	Jackson Racing	Nitrous Express
Bell Engineering	Powerdyne	Nitrous Works
Endyn	Rimmer	
FMAX		
HKS		
Hahn Racecraft		
Garrett Turbochargers		
Greddy Performance		
Knight Engineering		
RD Racing		
Rev Hard		
Turbonetics		
Turbo Engineering		
Turbo Performance		
XS Engineering		

Fig. 5-19: Hey, you don't have to swap out that classic Civic engine. Check out this 1200cc little monster with an early Reed cam, port and polished head, upgraded valves and valve springs, topped off by a Weber carb. Total horsepower output is 130. But remember—it's power to weight. This 1979 Civic tips in at only 1980 pounds.

be used sparingly. Don't be a knucklehead: although you can crank up the density to produce a 150-horsepower shot, it will likely let you do it only once. Then you'll have to spend time cleaning up the rubble that was once your engine.

With all this hoopla surrounding 10-second, quarter-mile Hondas, don't be totally sucked into overbuilding your street Civic, CRX or del Sol. Sure, going fast is fun and, when used intelligently, can even earn you some contingency money. You must do it for the lust of *speed*, however. Don't believe for a minute you're going to make money when you sell your built-up Honda. This is your passion, not your profession.

Power To The Pavement

Fig. 6-1: Getting the power to the pavement requires special components. For drag racing, the clutch and flywheel need to handle a mass amount of torque. As for shifting, the throws must be short and positive. Unlike in domestic applications, no manufacturer has stepped up to produce an in-line shifter for Hondas.

It's all about power, right? Not so, grasshopper. Whether you've got 200 street horsepower or a full-dog, 600 hp quarter-mile blaster, getting the power from will to thrill takes the right transmission, clutch, shifter and technique. Trust me, it doesn't make any difference what kind of a beast you've got under the hood if you can't get the power to the asphalt. We've got a good thing going now, so this chapter concentrates on getting the most from that good thing.

For the vast majority of import enthusiasts, what is housed under that molded plastic knob and metal stick poking up from the floorboard is a mystery, an aluminum casing filled with a baffling combination of cables, rods, gears, bearings, channels, myths and monsters. The extent of most people's knowledge is that when the car works the power is transported from the engine to the wheels. And, when it doesn't, the horrifying sound of metal grinding rings in the ears, and the vibration shutters up the shifter, stinging every nerve ending in the right hand and arm.

For my money, the transmission, clutch and shifter make all the difference in the world. Driving a car with a nice, short, positive shifter, a tight clutch and a solid feel in the gears is about as much fun as you're allowed to have outside of the NOPI Nationals.

For everything the del Sol had going for it when it was introduced (reasonable horsepower, innovative features and cutting-edge styling), it fell short of matching the Mazda Miata in the most important category—being fun to drive. Before reading on, take a ride to a local Mazda dealer and test-drive a Miata. It doesn't have to be a new model—any Miata with manual transmission will do.

Now that you've got it, how do you make it hook up? Trannys, clutches, LSD (not the drug) and other useful traction tips.

Welcome back. Did you have a good time? You should have. You can have a lot of fun driving a Miata. Straight out of the dealer's showroom the car is tight, quick and responsive—and, it has about the best-feeling shifter and transmission combination ever offered. Now compare this to your Honda Civic. Quite a difference. All factory Honda shifters have a long throw between gears. And while the transmission provides a clean, positive feel, the clutch feel is soft. Wouldn't it be a perfect world if you could combine the quick-shifting fun of the Miata with the power of your Honda engine? Welcome to a perfect world—and perhaps an even more perfect universe.

Once again, thanks to an aggressive automotive aftermarket, your factory transmission can have the feel and performance of Honda's racing heritage with the durability and day-to-day function you need for years of trouble-free operation. This chapter offers a focus not just on the components that make a Honda tranny feel and perform better but on the shifting techniques used by race car drivers to achieve optimum levels of speed and control.

The Clutch

We all know what a clutch does—or do we? The primary job of the clutch is to hold and distribute torque. Factory Honda clutch plates (manufactured by a Japanese company called Daikin) have a modest torque rate. This makes the pedal simple and easy to control, an ideal condition for everyday stop-and-go driving and parking-lot creeping. An internal diaphragm determines this torque-holding rate. Performance clutch plates are assembled with higher-rate diaphragms, allowing them to hold a higher amount of torque.

Performance clutch sets come in single- or twin-plate applications. Single-plate clutch sets can be installed with a choice of organic or cerametallic compositions.

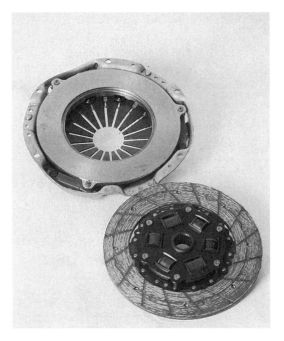

Fig. 6-2: For most street use the factory clutch and flywheel will work well enough. As soon as you bulk up the engine with 250 or more horsepower, however, it's time to start shopping for aftermarket replacements.

It is highly important to note that nearly all performance clutch sets begin life as factory Honda components. For the most part, aftermarket clutch sets are resurfaced units with higher-rate diaphragms. While these reworked units are a major improvement, we could identify only one clutch manufacturer, Exedy, which manufactures clutch sets especially for performance applications.

Single-plate clutch plates with organic composition are designed for everyday street driving. However, properly treated, these units can easily handle the weekend performance-driving activities of autocross and drag racing. Take note: these are for Civics with horsepower ratings up to 300.

The friction materials of organic or normal metallic discs are engineered to offer Civic owners improved pedal response without being harsh. This composition can also deliver long-term durability, even with weekly competitive use. One of the most important horsepower-aiding functions of a true performance clutch set is the reduction of inertia. This helps quicken the transaction of torque from the engine to the drive wheel(s). It is a general rule that the thicker the clutch plate, the greater the inertia. Organic clutch plates are usually the thickest of all aftermarket units, but they reduce as much as 20 percent of movement inertia over the factory stock clutch.

The next step up is a single-plate clutch with a cerametallic composition. These are designed primarily for racing applications. A good cerametallic clutch set will feature a more sensitive response factor over normal clutch plates. For drag racing or heavy-duty autocross Civics, this is a very positive upgrade, especially when engine power ratings get pushed up from 300-500 horsepower.

Cerametallic clutch materials are ultra-light weight due to reduced thickness of friction materials. Although thinner than normal clutch sets, the material is special-

Fig. 6-3: Exedy by Daikin offers high-performance clutch sets in both organic and ceremetallic composites.

ly developed to withstand the high torque felt under acceleration. By its reduced thickness and special tolerances, cerametallic clutch sets enable you to shift quicker and transport the torque-reducing traditional driveline losses.

For over-the-top performance applications, twin-plate clutch sets are the ultimate performance partner. These are designed for high-torque motorsports activities. However, unlike racing clutch plates for American V8 cars, twin-plate clutch plates that mate to Honda engines can be set up to deliver reasonable pedal pressure. This lighter pedal pressure helps ensure more accurate foot control, especially when launching. Twin-plate clutch sets can possess substantially more torque capacity than single plate clutch sets. On some units a choice of settings is available to best match the style and type of racing or preference.

One very important factor to consider before purchasing any high-performance clutch is price. Clutch or clutch/flywheel combinations are not cheap. As with every other performance modification you make, you should assess the need before making the purchase and spending the time to perform the installation. For most street-use Civics, the factory clutch will perform at an adequate level. When the stock Honda clutch begins to falter, then look into an aftermarket replacement. You'll find the performance items will require only a small upgrade in price, and installation efforts will be the same as if you swapped out the blown stock unit.

There are two types of flywheels designed for Honda Civics—steel and aluminum. The factory O.E. flywheel is made from steel. While extremely durable, it is also remarkably heavy. If you were to take two Honda flywheels and place them on each end of an iron bar, you'd never need to renew your membership to a health club or gym. The fact is that your stock flywheel is much heavier than you need, and the reasons for this are quite simple. First, the extra flywheel weight makes shifting easier and smoother for everyday driving. Second, steel is a low-cost material and steel flywheels can be produced far more economically than aluminum flywheels.

An aluminum flywheel offers a number of performance benefits over its steel counterpart. The most notable is that less power is needed to turn an aluminum flywheel because the energy usually needed to spin the steel flywheel is saved by an aluminum flywheel. This saved power can be used to turn the front tires and wheels. In addition to adding horsepower to the wheels, a lighter aluminum flywheel also relieves stress on the crank. The drawback to an aluminum flywheel is that the idle is not as smooth as with the heavier stock unit.

For the turbo performance geeks, an aluminum flywheel is a good horsepower investment. Because the lighter weight requires less energy to spin, turbo lag can be reduced as the engine more rapidly reaches optimum rpm range.

When shopping for an aluminum flywheel, check how the friction plate is secured to flywheel. Try to avoid units where steel or brass rivets are used. If possible, stainless steel rivets are preferred.

An old money-saving trick is to shave surface from a stock steel flywheel, but this is generally a poor choice. Remember, like all your engine and transmission components, the flywheel is a precision part. Simply shaving surface material will only serve to weaken the flywheel. Because it is the buffer for the force generated by the engine, weakening the flywheel can only result in failure.

The Differential

There has been a major trend to install limited-slip differentials (LSD) in Civics with high-performance engines. To get the power of the engine and the improved clutch to work at its peak capacity, a limited-slip unit is necessary. Installing an LSD is not going to be a cheap or easy process, but it is nevertheless something well worth doing.

Have you ever wondered why all the leading import performance magazines talk about the performance advantages of running with an LSD but never reveal how to install one? While installing an LSD unit in your Civic is a good thing, finding one is *not* such a good thing. Reason? They are not available as an aftermarket performance product, therefore your only complete option is to locate a factory unit from a dealer or a salvage yard.

The first step in locating a Honda-made LSD is to start the engine of your Civic, shift into gear and head directly for your local Acura dealership. This is where you'll find a parts department that will deliver the disturbing news. The only Honda-made LSD that fits easily into a Civic is one that comes from an Acura Integra GS-R. What makes the GS-R unit so special is that it works so well and installs without a great deal of special effort. What makes the unit so bad is the small number of Integra GS-R models that were produced, which makes successful salvage yard treasure-hunting difficult.

The Shifter

There is no market shortage of performance shifters—and with good reason: one drive around town in any Civic or CRX will convince you to perform a swap-out. The bent baseball bat Honda put through the floor feels like it has a mile-long swing. Remember that Miata test drive? If you do, then you know the shifting action you want from your Civic.

The all-important major difference between Mazda's Miata and Honda's Civic is that one is rear-wheel drive and one is front-wheel drive. This makes a difference on how the shift of torque is felt. In other words, you can make the shifting of gears feel just as tight, but the transfer of power will be felt up-front instead of under your seat.

Fortunately, all late-model Honda Civics and CRXs (1988 and newer) have manual transmissions with rod-style shifting rather than cable shifters. Rod-style shifter configurations allow for an easy installation of short-throw shifter kits.

There are two popular short-throw shifter product descriptions. One consists of a bracket that reduces the lever geometry. The other is an adjustable shifter that provides the options of changing the throw length and/or stick height.

The short-shift kit with brackets can cut the throw by as much as 40 percent over the factory shifter. This action quickens shifting and helps eliminate acceleration loss during gear changes. Because this product category uses the factory shifter, in most cases there is no need to remove the O.E. stick unit. A bracket-type shifter kit requires you to remove only the shaft rod from the stick. The bracket is the key to shorter shifts. Once the shift rod is removed, the bracket acts like an elaborate spacer that changes the throw length. The stick movement is shorter and the rod throw is changed accordingly.

The second option is the adjustable throw shifter. These kits are complete replacement units that displace the entire factory shifter shaft and ball unit.

Although replacing the entire shifter may sound complicated, it is usually an easy procedure. Honda designed the 1984-99 Civics with stock units that connect to a rod, which makes the connections on the transmission. This engineering design makes the job fairly straightforward. It is a task just about anyone with modest mechanical knowledge and a few hand tools can complete with relative ease, but it will require you to spend some time on your back under your car.

There are a number of good short-throw shifter kits available. For this chapter, two of the best-known name brands were tested—PaceSetter's Quick-Shift unit and B&M's Edge shifter. Comparing the PaceSetter and B&M shifters to the stock unit shows one of the most obvious improvements. The fac-

tory Honda shifter comes up from the rod connection and makes two bends, one aft and one up. The Pacesetter shifter makes only one 20-degree aft bend. The B&M shifter is completely straight, eliminating the bend altogether.

First, let's examine the PaceSetter shifter. The Quik-Shift unit allows you to adjust both the throw length and the stick height. This results in shorter shift throws and more precise gear changes. At the end of the shifter shaft is an "AdjustaBall," which allows you to dial in the shift throw. In some cases the throw can be as much as 80 percent shorter than stock. This shift ball is made from Delrin, a material developed for its low-friction qualities. You'll want to order the Quik-Shift with the optional durable polyurethane bushings, which will help ensure quick shifting for the life of the car. Remember the discussion on suspension? Polyurethane bushings resist nearly every type of contaminants, including gasoline and road salts. Therefore, the shift bushings will likely never wear out or break down like rubber or molded bushings.

After installation, you can adjust the shifter height to your personal hand position. This is an important feature because the proper hand and arm position helps you make those flick-of-the-wrist shifts we all desire.

B&M's Edge shifter design features a straight shaft that delivers improved leverage over the factory curve shaft. This one design enhancement reduces the travel between shifts by as much as two inches. Another impressive feature about the Edge shifter is the counterbalance added to the bottom of the shaft. Although the added weight is only three ounces, it dramatically changes the positive feel of each gear change.

In and of itself, the B&M Edge shifter is an improvement. However, to get the full benefit of the product you will need the "Shift Stabilizer" kit as well. This is a separate item, and, like a good shift knob, must be ordered independently from the shifter.

The Shift Stabilizer kit consists of aluminum shift-rod mounts that replace the

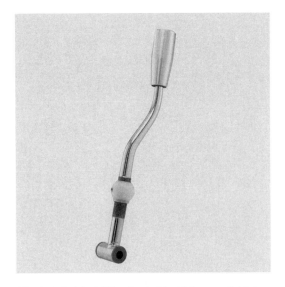

Fig. 6-4: Quick shifting is vital in all forms of driving competition—or just for fun. Short shifters, such as this unit from PaceSetter, can reduce shift throws by as much as 40 percent over the factory shifter.

factory rubber mounts. The aluminum mounts are rigid instead of compliant, thus eliminating flex under the pressures of speed or hard shifting. While installation is a bit more involved, it proves to be rewarding when it comes to hammer time. It also allows for fore and aft adjustment of the shifter to more precisely fit the ideal hand/shifter position.

Shifting the 1999 Project Donor Civic with the B&M unit required a bit more effort, but that added to the positive feel of each gear change, thus, making driving more enjoyable. After getting over the initial position change, you'll find yourself looking for opportunities to shift through the gears.

A short-shift device, whether a simple bracket or complete shifter kit, is a must-do installation. The price of these items is generally under $250, making this a cost-effective modification that not only will make your Civic a quicker commuter but also provide the all-important fun factor to every mile of driving.

For many years a large number of drag racers of domestic cars have found that automatic transmissions offer something manual transmissions can't—the ability to

not miss a shift. In 1996 Honda introduced an automatic transmission capable of handling more horsepower than the 1.6L engine produced. The CVT (continuously variable transmission) was the first Japanese automatic transmission to offer performance similar to that of the standard five-speed manual. The difference is that the CVT has only four forward gears. However, for drag racing, if your Civic gets into fifth gear, you've either missed a shift or driven off the end of the racetrack. Either one means you've lost the race.

The major drawback to an automatic transmission is the extra power needed to operate it. While the Honda CVT unit uses energy more efficiently than other automatics, a manual trans is still preferred by most racers.

In 1997 Honda introduced a hybrid automatic in its up-scale Prelude—a CVT automatic with Porsche-like "Triptronic" shifting capabilities. This is a sweet shifting- and power-stingy tranny that combines the best of both the manual and automatic worlds. It is something worth considering if you are making a VTEC swap from a Prelude to a Civic.

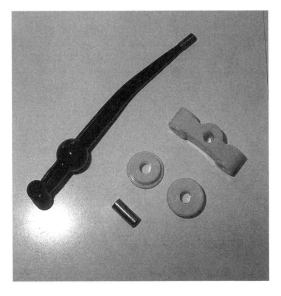

Fig. 6-5: Shifter kits, such as this Neuspeed unit, allow for more precise and positive gear changes

With your shifter in place and perhaps a new clutch and flywheel, it's time for a quick lesson on the fine art of speed-shifting. Speed-shifting is something we all like to do, but few do it well enough to make a difference. The real trick is discovering the ideal rpm range to maximize the powerband of your engine. In most 1.6L and 1.8L Honda engines the powerband comes on around 3,200 rpm. Therefore, when shifting you want to keep the red needle on the tach from dropping down beyond that point. This is where good coordination between your left foot and right hand comes into play.

With a little practice almost anyone can manage power-shifting from first to second or third to fourth. It's the transition from second to third where time and races are lost and where all those performance transmission products become factors.

A good shifter provides quicker, shorter throws from gear to gear. The lightweight flywheel brings the rpms back into the powerband quicker, and the clutch holds a greater degree of torque built up by the engine and released with improved precision. Thus it's not just about who can jam the gears the fastest; it's about making the best use of the power under the pedals—both clutch and accelerator.

Fig. 6-6: In 1996 Honda introduced its CVT automatic transmission. This four-speed option is a vast improvement over earlier Honda automatics. Although not preferred over the five-speed manual transmission, the CVT does allow for clean shifting with minimal loss of power.

STOP!: Improve Braking for Better Use of Horsepower

Fig. 7-1: Brake in, power out. This is the first rule of high-performance cornering.

on't make it go if you can't make it stop. This sounds like logical advice, yet few performance enthusiasts think about the braking system until the tail lights in front of them light up red brighter than a bordello in Amsterdam. The cold, hard truth is that bigger, more precise brakes not only help your Civic stop in a safer, more efficient manner, they can also make it stop faster and, of course, look better.

The vast majority of Civic, CRX and del Sol owners are saddled with a wary combination of front disc and rear drum brakes. In its factory configuration, this combination supplies adequate stopping distance and brake pedal control with minimal fade. During performance driving, stock brakes can overheat and lose as much as 40 percent of their effectiveness rating. This is mainly due to smaller disc calipers, solid rotors and ancient drum brake technology.

Remember the power-to-weight formula used to determine true horsepower results? Well, the same holds true for braking. Once again it comes down to the gross vehicle weight of your Civic to the force-resistance ratio of your brakes. This formula is radically altered by the factors of tires and wheel size and aerodynamic realignment resulting from adding styling components to the front valance and rear deck lid.

By now you've either completed or plan to add several performance modifications to your Honda Civic. If you're like 99 percent of all Honda performance geeks, the first steps you took were to bring the suspension and body closer together to reduce ride height and improve handling. This was followed by a more aggressive tire and wheel combination (see Chapter 3). This means that you've seen the small front disc brakes and

I don't need brakes . . . that's what guardrails are for. That's what happens when you have tons of horsepower, but no brakes. The do's and don'ts of improving your 60-0 times.

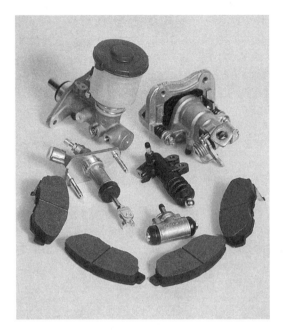

Fig. 7-2: Honda Civics have a host of components that play a part in effective braking. Items such as the master cylinder and booster will serve you well for the life of the car. Other items, such as the pads and lines, can provide low-cost performance.

unless you've got a 1988-89 CRX Si or a 1999-2000 Civic Si. A trip down Main Street can be eye-opening. By checking out the massive four-wheel 12-inch rotors of any late-model Corvette, Porsche, Viper or Acura NSX, you'll see where you want to be. But is all this expense and effort needed to bring your 3,000 pound Honda to a stop?

Bigger, stronger brakes are both a nice-to-have and a need-to-have problem. On the nice-to-have side, bigger brakes look better set inside larger wheels. On the need-to-have side, these brakes allow you to make better use of the extra horsepower you've added and to deliver a level of driver control and confidence you can't get with the factory system.

Perhaps the most frightening experience you'll ever have behind the wheel is brake fade or failure, which is why you'll want to consider a performance brake upgrade. It is also why you'll want to be very careful about the components you select. Quality, as in all things, should be the optimum feature. Don't purchase any brake components with price as an issue. If a better-quality system costs a bit more than you have, wait until you've got the extra green to make the purchase.

Performance braking isn't just about bigger rotors, multipiston calipers and exotic pads. It can be about small improvements to

realize how much smaller they seem with 17- or 18-inch wheels. And as for the eight-inch drum brakes in the rear, oh yea, they're an eyesore. It doesn't take a "rocket surgeon" to see the visual need for bigger front rotors and some kind of disguise for the rear drums,

Fig. 7-3: Most late-model Honda Civics are equipped with front disc and rear drum brakes. Behind 15- and 16-inch wheels the discs look and perform adequately. When you step up in wheel size and/or horsepower, it's time to start thinking about more efficient rotors and calipers.

Fig. 7-4: This is how most late-model Civics will look with factory brakes and 17-inch wheels. While the small front rotors still get some daylight, the rear drums provide no cosmetic advantage. Braking distance is slightly increased as well due to the extra inertia caused by the larger size and footprint.

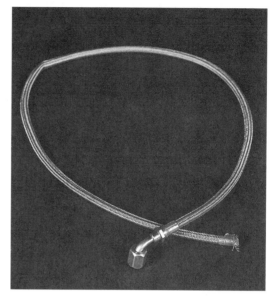

Fig. 7-5: Braided stainless steel brake lines are a must upgrade when installing high-performance brakes. These lines are highly resistant to weather, road salts and chemicals. They also won't crack as they age. But, most important, braided stainless steel lines won't expand and rupture under high-pressure use.

add that extra measure of stopping distance for the style of Civic you've created. After all, you may not need brakes that can stop on a dime and return nine cents in change. You may only require an upgrade that matches the performance improvements you have already made or are planning to make.

For example, with modest horsepower improvements and a common Plus Two tire and wheel upgrade, your Civic may need only performance brake pads. These pads will bring the 60-0 stopping distance back to that of the original pad with the factory pizza cutter tires and Ultra Slim-Fast wheels. Remember, those bigger, wider tires and wheels require more energy to stop as well as to turn.

For simple front disc brake pad upgrades to your Civic, you can use the factory caliper. You will need pads that provide a higher coefficient of friction, the force that slows down the wheel during braking. If you have ABS, this should not be affected by a simple pad replacement. The instant benefits of performance pads will be a slight improvement in

pedal control as well as a return to factory stopping distance. The durability and longevity of these pads are also superior to the factory Honda pads.

For the most part Honda brake pads hold up quite nicely for 50-60,000 miles. If your project is running over this mileage (or in multiples of 50,000 miles) remove and inspect the pads from the caliper. This is not a complicated procedure; it can be done in less than 60 minutes with a few common hand tools. A visual inspection of the pads usually shows wear. Like the wear bars found on tires, brake pads have similar built-in markings. If you are inclined to play it cheap, should the pads appear to have life left in them, simply place the pads back into the caliper, button up the assembly and go your merry way. However, since you got the pads out, why not spend $75, the average cost of upgrading the pads?

Current brake problems or future failure can be detected without removing the pads from the calipers. Take the 30-mile-an-hour

Fig. 7-6: For most street-performance Civics, a simple brake pad upgrade will deliver ideal performance.

stomp test. In an open area (such as an empty parking lot), accelerate to 30 miles an hour and let off the gas. Now lightly hold your hands on the wheel and depress the brake pedal slowly until the Civic's front noses over. The brakes should stop the car fairly straight and smooth. Now repeat the same test, only this time hold the wheel firmly and stomp the brakes. The feel or pull of the car should be as straight and true as the first test. Each time the pressure of the pedal should be firm and consistent. If the pedal reaches the floorboard, it is a warning sign; likewise, if the car dives forward or pulls to the left or right. Worn brake pads may also make that disturbing screeching sound. It is also good to note that noisy brakes can be the result of unwanted brake pad vibration, which can cause poor brake performance as the pad shutters inside the caliper, resulting in intermittent contact with the rotor. If the pads are still in good shape, this condition may require the caliper to be shimmed to restore an effective contact patch.

Replacing your front disc brake pads on a newer Civic is more than likely an overkill exercise. For the most part your factory braking system will serve you well, especially if you use your Civic for street use.

When you look at your Civic or del Sol's profile, you may determine that the rotors look microscopic positioned inside those oversized aftermarket 17- or 18-inch wheels. If this is the case, what you want is a set of 12-inch rotors. The problem is fitting these rotors to your factory caliper. This will require a bit of fabrication or a special hardware kit with repositioning brackets because Honda single-piston calipers do not have a wide enough mouth opening to accommodate thicker two-piece rotors. This is not a major stumbling block: AEM, CoolTech and Power Slot offer kits that allow you to upgrade the rotors while keeping the factory calipers.

The next step is to upgrade the rotors and calipers at the same time. A two-piston caliper provides more precise braking by increasing the balance of pressure put upon the pads to the rotors. This is the most cost- and performance-effective combination for performance-enhanced Civics.

The ultimate overhyped and oversold package includes four-piston calipers. Only the most powerful of race-built cars need this massive an upgrade. While you may enjoy the ego status of bragging about having race-prepared braking capabilities, it would be wiser to save the cash for suspension or seating improvements.

Speaking of overhyped—cross-drilled rotors enjoy a reputation that is largely unearned and unwarranted. In fact, most performance brake experts warn against installing true cross-drilled rotors. The reason for their concern? Structural weakness, of course. When brake rotors are drilled, the integrity of the plates can be compromised, which can result in the rotors developing stress cracks, leading to possible fragmentation under continued use.

So why do so many tuner shops push cross-drilled rotors? The theory is elementary. According to John Lewis of Baer Racing, one of the leading experts on high-performance brake systems, "On race cars where the rotors have a cherry red glow, the light show is caused by what is known as boiling off the binders." (This is a material in the brake pads that holds the friction

Fig. 7-7: These factory rotors were cross-drilled. While the myth is that this is to provide better braking, the reality is that cross-drilling your rotors can weaken them and cause the rotor to come apart.

material in place, very much like the glue that holds the entire pad together.) "When the binders boil off, it builds up a layer of gas between the pad and rotor. This acts like a shield, preventing the pad from striking the rotor," added Lewis.

In an effort to reduce this condition, race car engineers started drilling holes in the rotors to provide an exit route for these gases. When braking, the pads could "squeeze" the gas from the cross-drilled holes. Lewis went on to say that in "Today's brake pad technology, especially for street applications, boiling of the binders doesn't happen, or happens so rarely it is not even noticeable."

With new brake pad materials, the only other enemy of performance braking is heat. By reducing the heat buildup on the rotor surface, braking becomes more precise and effective. Holes drilled into the surface of the rotor are intended to dissipate heat quicker and provide vastly improved ventilation. The only problem with this is at highway speeds airflow through the holes is so slight that no additional effect is realized. However, if you've just got to have holes in your rotors, the key is to not drill the rotors but to cast these components with holes. This process allows the same levels of cooling and ventilation without the metal fatigue caused by drilling the rotors. In addition to cast-hole rotors, these are usually two-piece rotors with ventilation slots

to rapidly reduce brake rotor temperatures, should you have the opportunity to enter your Civic in competition at Le Mans, Daytona or Sebring.

Slotted rotors offer many of the same benefits as cast-hole rotors with one notable exception: they are much less expensive. Slotted rotors also reduce brake component gases. Most are of two-piece construction with ventilated slots separating the inner and outer plates for improved heat dissipation. For the money-to-performance ratio, slotted rotors beat cast-hole rotors every time. For improved street and sportsman racing brake performance, opt for slotted, ventilated

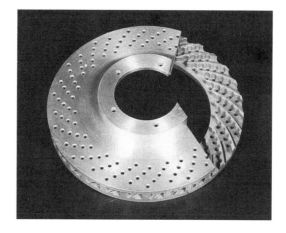

Fig. 7-8: If you are going to put up the big bucks for the ultra-high-performance look, make sure the holes are not drilled but, rather, are cast into the rotor.

Fig. 7-9: This is the high-buck brake package that is designed to help slow race cars from 170 mph straightaway speeds to 20 mph corners in seconds. As you can see, the calipers are four-piston and the rotors can be as large as 14 inches.

Fig. 7-10: Here's a more economical way to achieve better brake performance for the street and sportsman auto racing. Larger ventilated slotted rotors with high-performance calipers can reduce 100-0 stopping distance by as much as 30 feet.

rotors. The ideal street Civic setup is to have front-slotted rotors with two-piston calipers with high-performance pads. You will be rewarded with race-type appearance, precise braking control and improved durability.

Since only a few Civic, CRX and del Sol models were available with four-wheel disc brakes, most of us are saddled with rear drums. This is old-school technology that operates with a degree of proficiency but is one of the biggest points of dissatisfaction for nearly all Honda performance enthusiasts. Not satisfied with the status quo, many Civic owners have discovered an economical way to add rear disc brakes to their Civics. Nearing the final years of production, the 1988 and 1989 CRX Si models were equipped with four-wheel disc brakes. This system can easily be transplanted to most Civics. Unlike taking the rear-disc system from an Accord or Prelude, the CRX Si com-

ponents bolt on with no special fabrication necessary. In fact, in most cases the entire unit, swing arms and all, can easily be converted to late-model Civics.

The first trick is to find a 1988-89 CRX Si donor car. If you can't find one at any of your local salvage yards, check your local Auto Trader or newspaper classified section for a low-cost or non-op unit. Also check the local charities that deal in donation vehicles. Many times these groups pick up vehicles that will have more value to you as a multicomponent donor car. These charity groups hold regular fundraising auctions to reduce inventory. You'd be surprised the deals that can be had at these events.

After the CRX Si rear disc brakes are installed, you will likely experience an adjustment period as you get used to the manner in which the rear end ducks down or squats under heavy braking.

Fig. 7-11: In the summer of 1999, AEM introduced its MGS brake technology. This system allows you to upgrade your stock brakes with larger slotted rotors. Later you can add two- or four-piston calipers.

A major word of caution must accompany brake improvements or modifications: do NOT fall into the trap of relying on better brakes to get you out of poor driving decisions. Improved brakes are a tool to allow you to use your horsepower to a further degree. However, they are not saviors when the guardrail is staring you in the face. Once you've made a brake upgrade or modification, put about 1,000 miles of regular, unstrained driving on your car. This will allow you to get to know the feel of the pedal during day-to-day conditions. Then, when you really need it, your brain and right foot will have had a good deal of interaction with your Civic's new braking system.

A trip to your local drag strip will quickly demonstrate the need for heating up the drive tires before the tree turns to green. Heating up the drive tires increases traction and helps prevent tire spin. On rear-wheel-drive cars this is accomplished by installing a line-lock device. By engaging the line lock, the front brakes are locked on while the rear brakes are deactivated, allowing the rear tires to spin in the water box and heat up.

On Civics, CRX and del Sols, the front-wheel-drive configuration allows you to use the poor man's line lock—the e-brake. The emergency brake (or parking brake) is designed to lock up the rear wheels. By fully engaging the emergency brake lever, you can allow the front tires to spin and heat up for a more effective launch. The procedure is quite simple: just depress the clutch, put your Civic in first gear and engage the e-brake. Bring the engine revs up to about 2,500 rpm and slowly release the clutch while continuing to accelerate to about 4,000 rpm. The front tires will spin as they heat up. If you're doing this after wetting the tires in a water box, you can ease off the rpm levels a bit. Be sure to get only the front tires wet. As you back off the gas slowly, release the e-brake for a cheap adrenaline thrill.

Effective braking is a key to overall performance. If you have an opportunity to attend any performance driving school, one of the most important techniques you will be shown is how to use your brakes to optimize acceleration and cornering ability. On the street, your brakes are your safety net against wild animals, crazy drivers and errant objects.

Going In Style

Fig. 8-1: Showroom-fresh, our project Civic looks tame with 14-inch wheels, tons of wheel well gap and no styling add-ons.

At a recent import drag race event I ran across a friend who owns a very fast Civic. He has taken great care in selecting the components that have made his car one of the fastest street cars in the area. He has also devoted a great deal of money to make his Honda coupe what it is today. That's why I was puzzled when I didn't see a dial-in time scrawled in white shoe polish on his right side window.

I asked him why he wasn't running. Perhaps the turbocharger on the transplanted 1.8 was on the mend or he'd spun the shafts off the GS-R differential again. As major as these problems would have been, his answer was even more disturbing. "I didn't get my wing back from the painter," was his reply.

For all the technical knowledge and mechanical ability this Honda tuner geek had acquired over the past few years, he still believed that a wing on the trunk deck was going to make his car faster. Nothing could be further from the truth.

While styling packages and rear deck wings make a Civic, CRX or del Sol look more like a race car, none of these items do anything for the performance of the car. True, they make any of these Honda cars look sleek and race-like, but all they really do is add extra weight and physical bulk to the body.

When any of us think about exterior modifications, the first image that comes to mind is a body kit. At one time these items were called "ground effects" kits. This was in reference to the evolution European race teams had made in improving the aerodynamics of box-shaped German and British sedans. At the time it was discovered that by hanging a rubber-based

Let your body do the talking. Ground effects, wings, flares, windows, scoops and all the other cool body add-ons you can't live without.

Fig. 8-2: This front air dam is part of Xenon's 1999 Civic package. It utilizes Honda's lower mouth design with a molded-in grille.

strip along the lower panels of the body sides the air would funnel to the back of the car rather than exit out the sides. This reduced body "lift" and allowed the car to achieve better road adhesion, a technique that was used as far back as the mid-1960s on ultra-high-powered American Cam-Am-style cars to literally suck the car to the track. Later the science was refined to incorporate the ground effects into the body-styling.

Leaving no stone unturned, observant and innovative small-car street-performance buffs picked up on the trend. Soon many Datsun 510s, Toyota Corollas and Celicas were sporting flaps down the side and makeshift front air dams. Not long after, the trend grew from these simple strips into a multimillion dollar industry.

Today manufacturers refer to their products as styling packages rather than as ground effects kits. No longer offered in primitive rubber striping, these highly stylish and carefully designed packages are made from either fiberglass or polyurethane.

A basic styling package consists of four pieces: A front air dam, two side skirts and a rear valance. Matching rear deck wings are optional in the kit and are usually mandatory for street styling, albeit for appearance rather than function.

The main job of a styling package is to extend the bodyline closer to the road, thereby giving the car a more substantial and track-like appearance. In some applications, the styling actually delivers something that should have been engineered into them in the first place—better airflow. Airflow is used on race cars to create downforce on the car, helping to provide improved handling at high speed. This is perfectly well and good, except for one important factor: your Civic, CRX or del Sol will never achieve the speeds necessary to realize truly effective airflow downforce.

The bottom line is that the true function of a body kit is to make the car look sexier. There is nothing wrong with making your car look better—in fact, that's a primary goal

Want a Civic that will kick asphalt on BMWs, try this 260 horsepower Jackson Racing Si. A few laps on the high banks of California Speedway was very convincing.

This is a good representation of a clean, classic panel scheme—saturated green with multiple overlays, highlighted by pinstripes.

Here's a 1999 Si featuring a combination of tear-away panels with Super Touring race influences. This entire vinyl job was done in less than 12 hours.

A slick combination of street and sport is the theme of this del Sol. Done completely in vinyl, note how the headlights got the subtle treatment. The bold blue-over-white checkered flag effect brings the eye to the bottom of the vehicle, adding to the lower, track-like appearance.

Here is the difference between paint and vinyl. This wild panel job is made possible by hours of work. These graphics were laid out in multiple over-lays. Before spraying the candy colors, a base coat was applied. Over the candies are layers of clear. The entire job is color-sanded before being buffed to a deep finish. This is a first-class, show-winning paint job.

This reverse scallop job looks great, but it required the owner to address the red engine bay.

For the past five years the CRX has been well on its way to becoming a cult car. The clean, slick appearance and functional nature is the foundation for all that Honda stands for. This sweet version features a clever reverse scallop paint scheme.

Aggressively laid-back is this CRX with a go-fast appearance and an engine to match.

Smooth as silk. This is the blueprint for thousands of street prepared Civics.

Tear-away panels work well on Civics. This coupe carries the colors onto the brake calipers, brake drums and ground-effect grilles.

For racing, the only luxury is standing on the top step of the winner's podium.

One of the best Honda cars to start a project from is a CRX Si. The four-wheel disc brake package is a favorite transplant item for late-model Civic builders.

Eibach's Project Civic was one of the first tricked out Asian compacts to make the pages of Motor Trend. The paint scheme was developed long before Super Touring cars came to America.

Not every Honda project needs to be big bucks. This older red hatchback was put together for under $6,000, including the cost of the car.

Honda SOHC engines can be built to deliver very usable street power. A few well-selected bolt-ons and you can easily get 100–110 horsepower at the front wheels.

How about 375 horsepower performance with street car reliability. Turning up the boost will bring bigger numbers.

Doug Starbuck was one of the first big time custom painters to zero in on the Honda movement. His CRX paved the way for many who would follow.

A trick street car interior that is a little bit race and a little bit a show.

This is one sweet Civic coupe. The silver and candy orange is a striking combination. The 18-inch wheels and trick body treatments doesn't hurt either.

Ty Tipton's has become a Honda legend with his second generation Civic racer. In roadracing events, he consistently passes Ferraris and Porsches.

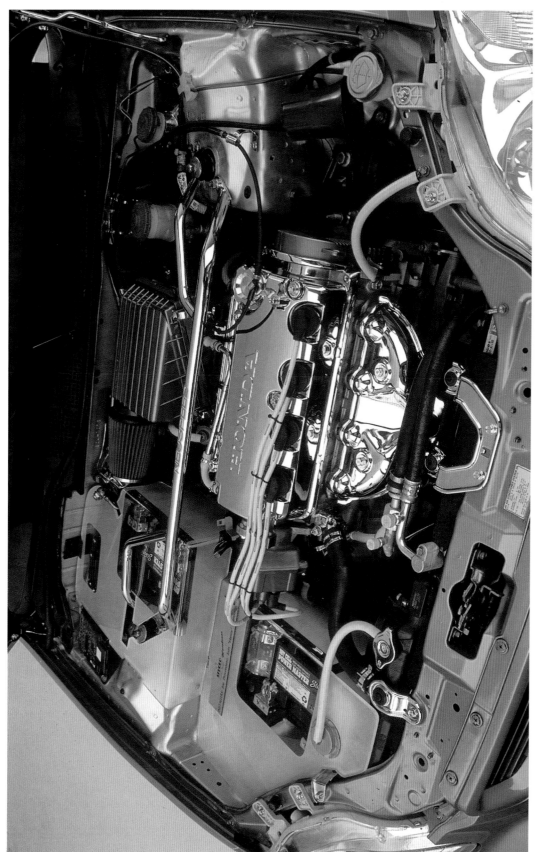

All show and no go. This 1.6L was built to win at the shows, not the strip.

Oscar Jackson gained a reputation of being a Beemer eater with this early hatchback. This car could also run circles around Porsches and Corvettes at solo events.

Fig. 8-3: This 1997 EX coupe features a more aggressive Kaminari kit with an extended front deck. You've got to be careful of parking lot tire-stop blocks as well as curbs with this kit.

when we begin to trick out a Civic. Even the guys who prime their Civics, lower the stance and keep the steel wheels do this as a status job. How many Civics have you seen running around town with a blown-out exhaust system with a six-inch tip, and dull paint with sponsor stickers plastered on the sides of the car? This is a styling trend all its own, with no difference in the owner's motivation than the Civic owner who hangs a body kit and bolts on 17-inch tires and wheels. But more on this later.

The first step in selecting a body kit is research, heavy-duty research. There are dozens of kits available. What you want is a high degree of styling with an equal dose of quality. Fine quality should be as primary a consideration as styling. All body kits look good in ads, catalogs and brochures. Trust me, I've produced enough sales literature over the years to choke a Formula One intercooler. Anything can be made to look and sound like a million-dollar product; what's going to make or break the process is fit and finish. A kit that is well-designed, manufactured and installed correctly will appear as if the Civic came that way from the secret Honda race car factory. A poorly made kit will look like it was an afterthought, as it hangs on the car like a wet extra-large T-shirt on a 98-pound weakling—nothing but gaps and seams.

There are several considerations when choosing a body kit. First, look at the front air dam. Nearly all have a lower line that incorporates a wide-mouth opening. In theory, this is to allow for more air to reach the cooling system, when in fact it also allows for more road debris to enter the fins of the radiator, oil-cooler or air conditioning condenser. If you select one of the kits with a wider mouth-opening, also inquire if there is a debris screen available to fit the kit.

To help direct air into your aftermarket cold air induction system, a few designers have engineered a pathway on the right side of the mouth. This pathway forces air to the area where a long-pipe intake is located. Increased airflow is also vital to turbochargers that run intercoolers.

The second feature about the front air dam is the lower ports. In race cars these ports are used to duct air to the brakes. Most street versions show these as an ideal location for auxiliary driving lights. What you do with these ports will depend on the style of Civic you want. If you choose to use these ports to vent your Civic's front brakes, you will need to create a duct that runs from the ports to the areas near the brakes. This material can be as simple as the duct used to vent your household clothes dryer.

Many use the lower front ports to install lights. Most lighting companies, such as

Fig. 8-4: True performance enthusiasts find ways to modify aftermarket air dams to allow for improved airflow to vital areas. For Ty Tipton's full-road race Civic, he engineered the right panel opening to flow air into the intake while the holes on the right cool the supercharger. Also note the thin slits to channel air to the brakes.

PIAA and Catz, design lights to fit into varying size ports. In most cases this will require you to drill and mount the lights, run electrical lines and install a switch. It can be a time-consuming job for items you rarely use.

Fig. 8-5: One low, lean CRX with all the exterior tricks. The front air dam drops the body-line nearly six additional inches, making this two-seat Honda a real grass cutter.

However, these lights do look good inside the ports and will serve a purpose when you drive at night on dark roads or, if you install fog lamps, when better visibility is necessary during inclement weather.

On late-model Civics the front air dam either replaces or completely caps the original front bumper, which makes the fit and finish even more of an issue. The new styling body panel must mate up to the fenders and hood as if it were an original factory component. This means the gaps in the body seam should be consistent from side to side.

Side skirts extend the body line closer to the road. Styles vary from subtle to gaudy: it's all a matter of personal taste. A word of caution: trendy styles come and go. (Remember the Testarosa-style side fins?) Once you've attached a set of side skirts to your Civic, taking them off or replacing them with another style will be costly. It is better to lean toward the conservative side rather than latch onto the 90-day-wonder trend. This will ensure you will still be happy with the look of your Civic in a year or more.

Rarely are side skirts designed to work in harmony with fender flares. If you're going to swell the fenders, don't waste time and money on a complete styling package that includes the side skirts.

Fig. 8-6: How about something on the wild side? Southern California custom painter Doug Starbuck went the radical route with his CRX front air dam. The custom-made piece features a deep-set mouth and functional cold-air scoop.

Fig. 8-7: This 1993 coupe features a full Xenon kit. Note how smoothly the side skirts carry the line from the front air dam. Also note the trick way the driving light ports are frenched into the grille opening.

All styling packages come with a rear valance. This item is necessary to complete the new styling flow of the Civic/CRX/del Sol. However, this is the one piece of the package that creates the most problems. Most manufactures mold the valance to accommodate the factory exhaust tip or one slightly larger in diameter. We tend to install tips two to three inches larger than stock. This causes a fitment dilemma that translates into either selecting a tip smaller than desired or altering the opening or area des-ignated for the exhaust exit. The problem can be avoided by going back to the rule of planning your construction in subtraction. Plan out your exhaust system needs prior to selecting a styling package. However, install the styling package before performing the exhaust work. This will minimize the possibility of fitment problems from the muffler, exhaust pipe or tip size interfering with the installation of the rear valance.

Although the rear valance is the least fashionable of the four basic styling compo-

Fig. 8-8: Sigma's 1994 Civic kit also wraps around in a continuous styling line. This kit is a bit more conservative than most, making it popular with Honda dealerships of that time. This is why you'll find many used Civics with Sigma kits.

Fig. 8-9: Remember when? Here's one from the archives—a 1992 Civic hatchback with Testarosa influences. This was the big styling trend in the early to mid-1990s. Today you'd be ripping the side panels off the car. A good lesson on how fast flash can turn to trash.

nents, it plays a very important part. After all, if you get into a speed contest with someone else (like that would never happen), the back of your car is what you want your competition to see. However, the styling issues of a rear valance are more than just about appearance; they can and should be about function.

"Function," is the key word. Most manufacturers of styling components fail to design a rear valance with a form that can actually supply a Civic, CRX or del Sol with usable airflow qualities. It appears the goal is to simply match the lower body line of the car, which means the bottom of the rear valance pushes down and sweeps out. This styling, while appearing consistent with the side skirts, does not deliver any lower aero-

dynamic advantage. It may cause handling and performance problems, as it can create greater drag and airflow lift. The line should in fact sweep under the car, rounding the lower look of the Civic's rear end. This effect will provide for the airflow to easily escape with less rear-end lift because the air slides under the car rather than pushing up on a flat lower lip. In a sense, the rounded line makes the underbelly more aerodynamic or slippery to the passing air.

There are two materials used in the making of styling packages. The older of the two is fiberglass, a material that has a workable advantage because it is easy to prep, smooth and paint. Fiberglass holds its shape under highway and greater speeds and is impervi-

Fig 8-10: Xenon had the right idea when its designer crafted the 1993 Civic rear valance. You can see how the air travels under and through the body panel rather than pushing against it. The area for the exhaust tip is large enough to accommodate up to a four-inch boomer.

ous to the weather. It does have some glaring weaknesses: for one thing, it can get very brittle over time, and it does not handle road hazards, curbs, speed bumps and minor traffic accidents very well.

The other commonly used material is polyurethane, a highly pliable compound that can be bumped, twisted and smacked and will return to its original shape. It is lighter in weight than fiberglass and is easier to install. The downside is it is more expensive to purchase and paint (a flex agent additive to the base paint coat is required). However, body shops and auto painters find that very little if any prep work is necessary to paint urethane body parts.

A third material that has popped up recently is carbon fiber, an extremely light-

Fig. 8-11: This rear valance is part of the Xenon 1999 Civic styling package.

Fig. 8-12: Kaminari was one of the first manufacturers to build high-quality styling kits. This 1990 sedan is still in style a decade after it was designed.

Fig. 8-13: After a brief absence from the compact car arena, Kaminari returned to the styling wars in 1995. The company has resisted the lure of polyurethane and still make its kits from fiberglass. This del Sol kit shows the styling potential of Honda's forgotten two-seater.

weight material used on many race cars. At the 1998 SEMA Show (the Specialty Equipment Market Association Show is the annual convention and trade show for the automotive aftermarket industry), one company introduced a carbon fiber hood for Civics. Although crude and poor in quality, it did make a breakthrough in both styling and performance components. Carbon fiber as a material for styling packages is a long way off. The material is too fragile and expensive for everyday Civic use.

All this airflow science brings us back to rear deck wings. In the old days (late 1960s and early 1970s) these trunk lid extensions were called spoilers or airfoils. This term stemmed from the way they cheated the wind, causing downforce on the rear of the car.

Downforce is important to maintaining both traction and road adhesion. What?

Aren't traction and road adhesion the same thing? No, not when it comes to rear deck wings. Originally, oversized spoilers were designed for rear-wheel-drive cars. By increas-

Fig. 8-14: This is how a race Civic's rear deck wing works. See how the pitch of the wing is extreme, especially compared to the rear deck additions seen on the street.

Fig. 8-15: A Si with a functional wing. The airflow runs down the sloped rear window and onto the extended wing, if you could only get it going fast enough to actually work. The rear valance suffers from restricted exhaust port disease.

Fig. 8-16: The modest elevated rear deck wing designed for Civic in the mid-1990s has influenced an entire generation of car buyers. Today every make and model of new car comes with an optional rear deck wing—made popular by Civic enthusiasts.

ing downforce the drive wheels were pushed down onto the pavement, helping prevent any possible loss of driveline push. Your Civic, CRX or del Sol is front-wheel drive, therefore the scientific design of a rear deck wing for traction purposes is wasted—unless you stick a wing over the front wheels.

This brings us to road adhesion. A rear deck wing can deliver improved road adhesion, thus keeping the rear tires from slipping out from under the car as the front axles pull the car around the track. However, the speed necessary to bring this physics lesson into play is usually greater than you'll experience on a normal run around town. Where you could feel the effects of rear downforce is on a sweeping highway on-ramp when you need to accelerate and turn at the same time. (Use this reason as your justification for installing a rear deck wing.)

There are many different styles of rear deck wings. From small "flips" to massive super wings, the selection process can be mind-boggling. When all is said and done,

Fig. 8-17: Honda has gotten into the after-market accessories game by offering two rear deck wings for the newest Civic. This is the "High Wing," coming right from the dealer's parts department.

most of us are going to go for form over function. Wings that make contact with the trunk lid from side to side provide better usable airflow than wings that are elevated over the deck surface. The super-wing style started decades ago so as to use the air that flows over the top of the car to push down on the rear. This wing was made famous on Dodge Daytona Chargers and Plymouth Superbirds used in NASCAR racing in 1970-71. Before that, however, Jim Hall was using overhead wings on his Chaparral race cars. Hall made his wings adjustable to take advantage of both cornering and high-speed straightaway airflow. The driver could adjust the wing's pitch while driving. The Daytona and Superbird wings were fixed to grab the air and create traction and road adhesion.

If you look at these wings, you'll notice how the front of the wing is narrow and gets wider as it goes back. This is to cut through the wind to take better advantage of the downforce qualities and reduce drag-and-lift properties as much as possible. Before purchasing an elevated rear deck wing, make sure the air will flow in an efficient manner. And while you will likely never reach the speeds necessary to bring airflow downforce into full effect (at over 130 mph), you can at the very least look and sound like you understand the physics of the subject.

There are other styling items that can be justified with performance qualities. Take a sunroof, for example. To nearly everyone, a sunroof is an item installed to make driving more fun. And, indeed, a sunroof can enhance the driving experience, but it can also make your Civic or CRX handle better. How, you ask? The answer is structural rigidity. In Civics, especially late-model units, the overall stretch of the roof (from side to side) can be stiffened with a sunroof install. This reduces the flex length during hard cornering. I know it sounds strange, but it is completely logical.

Fig. 8-18: How about a functional wing for the roof? This spoiler sunroof from SFC may not offer any aerodynamic advantages, but it does increase the roof's structural rigidity. This translates into reduced body flex and could improve handling. Okay, it's a stretch, but good justification for having a sunroof installed.

There are other items that serve no practical purpose and, for that matter, deliver only questionable styling benefits. Still, these items are marketed down our throats. The most glaring of these are tinted or smoked headlight and tail light covers.

Looking at your restyled Civic is one thing—learning to live with it is another. There are new driving habits you need to establish to accommodate your Honda's lower, sleeker stance. When your car was at factory height (nosebleed caution), driveways, speed bumps and small road hazards were never a concern. After lowering the car with performance springs these items became small inconveniences. Now, with the addition of a styling package that lowers the body line by as much as six inches, these once-friendly obstacles encountered everyday are now enemies. To avoid damage, or at least minimize the damage, here are a few basic rules to live by:

Approach driveways at an angle. Front air dams take a beating from attempting to enter and exit straight on. By taking on a driveway cutout at an angle (usually at about 20 degrees) you allow your Civic to lift the edge closest to the driveway. In a way, it's like rolling over the driveway rather than onto it. This also works for speed bumps.

Take it slow. By slowing down as you enter or exit a driveway or speed bump you reduce the measurable energy the springs and dampers absorb and will recoil. (See Chapter 3.) When you reduce the compression and recoil of the suspension you keep the car in a more neutral stance.

Fig 8-19: Could this be today's trend? Take a look at the over-the-top scoops on this Wings West Civic kit. The side skirts, rear valance and roof wing stay on the conservative side but the air dam is massive and on the edge. Also note the fiberglass hood treatment.

Fig. 8-20: Xenon has been in the styling game since the ground-effects days. This Gen 3 kit uses driving light ports in the air dam and picks up the styling trick on the side skirts. Note how exposed the radiator grille is to road debris.

Fig. 8-21: An early A&A kit for the CRX. Clean, smooth lines with functional brake ports in the air dam.

Dive and drive the dips. Road and drainage dips are more subtle than driveways and speed bumps, but they can still cause damage. One method is to dive into the dip using the brakes and gas out, hitting the accelerator just as you are descending into the dip. The surge of power lifts the front of the Civic, gaining a few inches of clearance. If you've installed a supercharger, watch that you don't accelerate too much or you'll be doing a *Dukes of Hazard* wannabe scene.

Look ahead and plan ahead. Road hazards are something you can't predict or plan for—they just pop up, sometimes out of nowhere. The best way to avoid these unknown minefields is to minimize the potential by always keeping your options open. For example, never drive behind a big rig or lifted pickup truck. These guys spray rock, asphalt and crap all over the road. Plus, the height of these vehicles blocks any forward visibility. I apply this same rule to larger sport utility vehicles. I also use any extra power my 1.8L engine has to get away from VW buses (you don't want to get stuck behind one of these things on an incline). Also, if you can't see the head of the driver in front of you or he or she is wearing a 1950s-style hat and has either gray, white, or no hair, get in front of this driver as soon as you can (because they are unpredictable, old-school drivers). By leaving your options open you can switch lanes to maneuver around problems. And

Fig. 8-22: Here's another golden oldie. The owner of this '92 hatch adapted, overcame and improvised. To get around the small holes for the exhaust tip, he installed dual tips on each side. The right side is functional while the left tips are dummies.

always remember debris never travels alone. Where there is one piece there will be more. All that fragmented tire tread on the road comes from big rigs blowing out their recapped tires. Just because it's rubber doesn't mean it's soft. At 60 mph that stuff can rip the front air dam clean off—or at least carve a gaping hole.

Styling packages will add a more sophisticated appearance to your Civic, CRX or del Sol. Just keep in mind they are not performance-enhancing products. You will need to plan ahead to ensure that the tires, wheels and suspension components you select will work with the body panels. Remember that the styling package will lower the body line by several inches. If you go too low with your suspension before the styling components are installed, you may find yourself dragging or smacking the road even under normal driving conditions. So, as with everything else discussed in this book thus far, the key is to plan ahead and make intelligent, informed decisions.

Interior Designing

Fig. 9-1: It isn't any wonder that some tricked-out Civic owners/builders leave the interior alone. Here's a nice, clean interior of a Civic hatchback in black and gray—nothing special, but it's clean and functional.

chapter 9

Take a seat—or two. While you're at it, grab a steering wheel and gearshift knob. And don't forget a few gauges and a roll cage. After all the work you've done to make your Civic accelerate faster, handle quicker and look better, you now need to focus your attention on the interior.

Interior designing for Civics, CRXs and del Sols can be any artistic vision you can imagine. The only boundaries you are confined by are between the door panels and glass. From crushed velvet to stripped and stark, inside the metal body shell is an open canvas ready for your creativity.

With the exception of the del Sol, Civics and CRXs were originally designed with boring yet functional interiors. The set and angle of the gauges are installed for easy, at-a-glance viewing. The seats are made to accommodate a variety of—well, seats. The patterns are generally conservative, selected as to neither attract nor revolt mass consumers. However, the evolving discussion in Chapters 1 through 8 is based on the premise that *your* Civic is not meant for the masses. Therefore, since you're going to spend a lot of time looking at your car from the inside, it's best to construct an interior package that reflects the personality of the car—in other words, one that also plays well with the exterior and performance features of the car.

When it comes to either a show or go Civic, CRX or del Sol, the interior is usually the one area where the allocation of construction funds are diverted away and given to parts and pieces that make the car move faster or look better. However, a well-executed interior plan can make your car go faster and handle better. At the very least, the interior makes the car

It's what's inside that counts. Creating a comfort zone that allows you to go fast and feel good.

Fig. 9-2: Here's a 1999 Civic with the a custom leather package, the ultimate in luxury. Classic Soft Trim offered up this design, available at most Honda dealers at time of purchase. CST also has installation facilities in most major metropolitan areas.

comfortable and enjoyable to drive. The construction of the interior should be given just as much attention as any other part of the car. This chapter covers the vital interior components: seating, carpeting, belts, race-and-roll cages and gauges and accessories.

Seating

This is as good a place as any to start the personalizing of your interior. Unlike other areas of your project, there are no basic kits for Civic interiors; therefore, what you do inside may be more personal and character-reflecting than the exterior paint, wheels or performance. The seats or seating material you select will set the tone for the rest of the interior. You can choose to keep the original front seats or perform a bucket swap. Either way, you can improve the appearance and drivability of the car.

Each front seat is connected to the floor via two runners (the tracks that allow you to adjust the seat fore and aft). The runners are designed specifically for each model to contour to the shape of the floor pan. Each seat has a left and right side runner, which can be the same length but differ in the shape and placement of the

Fig. 9-3: Gutting the interior is one way to make a statement. This is a low-bucks solution that allows you to reinstall the factory interior when and if you want. This hatch was gutted from stem to stern, leaving only the center console, dash and spare tire.

Fig. 9-4: This del Sol builder went the full-on custom route. The seats are dual-tone tweed fabric. Note how the rear cabin panel and console were covered to match.

Fig. 9-5: Here's the rear storage compartment of the same del Sol. The tweed theme carries through and is accented by the polished rear strut bar.

mounting pad. Each runner is fastened to the floor by four bolts. Therefore, to remove the front seats you need only remove these bolts and lift the seats and runners out as single units.

Because the seats are so easy to remove, they become prime candidates for replacement. Civic and CRX owners have been blessed by the aftermarket and have many choices when it comes to bolt-in seating. For del Sol owners, the selections are not so plentiful.

Seat selection is very important. You need a seat that provides good support for your shoulders, back, hips and legs. You need

good lateral support for cornering, comfort for long drives, easy in-and-out access for everyday functioning and compatibility with either existing and aftermarket seat and harness belts.

The original seats in most Civic and CRX models are somewhat flat in construction and offer little lateral support during aggressive driving. The padding is adequate for day-to-day operation. However, if you're working with an older Civic, the foam under the surface material may be breaking down. This is usually evidenced by the driver's seating surface sagging to the left (this side of the driver's seat takes the most abuse over its life-

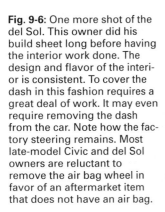

Fig. 9-6: One more shot of the del Sol. This owner did his build sheet long before having the interior work done. The design and flavor of the interior is consistent. To cover the dash in this fashion requires a great deal of work. It may even require removing the dash from the car. Note how the factory steering remains. Most late-model Civic and del Sol owners are reluctant to remove the air bag wheel in favor of an aftermarket item that does not have an air bag.

time). If the driver's seat structure is breaking down, this is an ideal excuse for justifying a seat swap. Purchasing an aftermarket performance seat costs about the same as reconstructing the original seat. Plus, there is only minimal downtime with an aftermarket seat swap, while reconstructing the original means several days at an auto upholstery shop. You do, however, have the option of picking up a used seat at a salvage yard. If you decide to do this, look for a passenger-side seat that you can remove from the runners and attach to the driver's side runners. Passenger seats are usually in much better shape because they have been used for fewer passenger miles.

Replacing a worn seat or seats in an older Civic is a short-term fix. What you really want is an interior that reflects the overall theme of the car. To get what you want means more than just a seat swap. In fact, swapping seats to aftermarket items may cause more problems than it solves.

Some aftermarket seat manufacturers work hard to use materials that come close to matching the color and texture used by Honda. However, for the most part, *close* to the original color is about as good as it gets. With the exception of black, rarely does a gray color, such as aftermarket seat, match the color of the original. There is an even greater contrast in tan or brown shades.

If it is black you're working with, you can select seats with a color insert to contrast the abyss. Planned in advance, you can use this as a springboard for the rest of the interior components. Door panels can be stitched or sewn with beading that matches the seat-insert color. Gauge faces can be installed to match, as can accent items such as the paint for the window cranks and door handles.

It all starts with the seats. There are several different styles: lowbacks, highbacks, sport and racing. Lowback seats are generally used in customs and offer little or no driving advantage over factory seats. Highbacks are usually adapted from other makes or models.

Aftermarket manufacturers concentrate their efforts on sport and racing seats. Sport seats are a good compromise between the factory seats and racing seats. Generally speaking, aftermarket sport seats come with pre-drilled holes to attach the factory runners. Lower-priced sport seats may require you to mark and drill holes to accommodate the runners, although, depending on how old your Civic is, you may need to perform this work no matter what manufacturer produces the seats. Racing seats will deliver the best support but are lacking in comfort for day-to-day driving. Racing seats are also far more difficult to access because the high

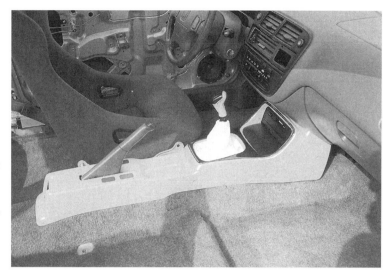

Fig. 9-7: Here is a street version of a race interior. The owner of this Civic hatch gutted the car of all the creature comforts. The race seat is devoid of comfort but loaded with high-speed support. Oddly enough, what's missing is racing harness belts and a roll bar.

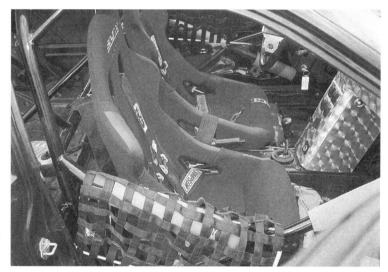

Fig. 9-8: Real race cars need functional seating, restraints and instrumentation. Ty Tipton's full-race Civic features a full-cage system, racing seats and an aluminum dash with all the necessary gauges.

bolsters and side structures often require gymnastic maneuvers to enter and exit.

It is very important to do your homework when selecting seats. Many aftermarket seats will deliver a seat platform higher than the original factory seat, so when you mount the seat onto the Honda runners you may find its position too high for your taste. This will also have an effect on your ability to control the car. High-end aftermarket seating manufacturers such as Recaro and Sparco include runners specially designed for more popular Civic applications. These runners are the key to proper placement and adjustments.

Sport seats are a minimum of two pieces designed to provide reclining positions and forward tilt for access to the rear seat. These seats can also include a variety of adjustments. A racing seat is one piece which means the seating position is fixed in place. The only adjustment is either forward or back. Racing seats are made to be used with harness belts. These are great for competition but can be a hassle if you use your Civic for everyday driving. Sport seats work in conjunction with your factory belts but are not always compatible with harness belts.

The seating situation is not a cut-and-dried issue. The best way to select aftermarket

Fig. 9-9: Going racing? You can in this '97 hatchback. The Sparco seat and racing belts are for solo driving. Note the integrated full cage.

seats is to test them out, literally, by the seat of your pants. Most tuner shops have a few seats on display. At major events, such as the NOPI Nationals, Hot Import Nights or SEMA's International Auto Salon, seat manufacturers will have complete lines on hand for you to test to your heart's content.

When you shop for seats, be sure to ask the sales representative these questions:

- Are the runners included?
- What material is used to make the frame?
- How long does the warranty or guarantee last?
- Will the seats work in harmony with factory or harness belts?
- How adjustable are the height and recline positions?
- What is the overall width of the seat?

The seat width is very important. If the seats are too wide they will not allow for the

doors to close, and they may crowd the center console and make shifting difficult.

Another problem aftermarket seating can present is matching or contrasting with the rear bench seat. You have several rear seat options:

Remove the rear seat. This will require you to construct a panel so as not to have a direct line of sight into the trunk area. In many cases, the rear seat acts as a border separating the interior cabin from the trunk. When you remove the rear seat the crossmembers that stiffen the body from side to side are fully exposed. This is only a problem on coupe and sedan Civics. CRX and del Sol models as well as Civic hatchbacks generally don't present these concerns. Two common ways to separate the interior from the trunk is by cutting a 1/2-inch piece of plywood and covering it in matching automotive-grade carpeting. A second solution that works for Civics with a race flavor is to use sheet aluminum as a border. You can carry over this theme to the door panels and rear windowsill as well.

Recover the rear seat. Aftermarket seat manufacturers have forgotten that rear seats exist. Therefore, you will need to seek out an auto upholstery shop that can match the front seat material. This is where leather or vinyl becomes an advantage over fabric.

Live with the original rear seat. While this is the easiest option, it will start to grate on you whenever you show your car.

When you make an upgrade seating investment, you want it to be a long-term situation. Comfort, performance and longevity are important issues.

Door Panels

After selecting the seat that best suits your Civic, it is normal to want the door panels to

Fig. 9-10: Back to reality. This Civic tuner used a few cans of red spray paint to accent the factory gray throughout the interior. The seat rail covers, gauge carrier, vents, speaker grids, door panel inserts and seatbelt attachment covers were all sprayed red. Quick, effective and cheap.

match, but seat manufacturers rarely offer door panels and seats as a package. Therefore, it is going to be up to you to either find a matching material or have a professional auto upholsterer rework the panels. There are also other options.

First, lets explore the do-it-yourself option. Many major metropolitan areas have outlets for professional auto and furniture upholsterers. These stores often sell to the public. But don't expect a lot of friendly advice or customer service people who will walk you through the process. This job is going to be up to you, and it's not that hard to get in over your head.

In older Civic and CRX models the door panels are easy to cover. It most cases you don't even have to remove the factory vinyl. In fact, the factory design works in your favor by adding some shape and dimension to the job. To re-cover your door panels, first install the seats. Remove the right door panel to measure the amount of material needed to do the re-covering job. You must remove the window crank and molded bay of the interior door handle release. The window crank is held on by either a center screw or by a circle clip. If you come upon a circle clip, you need only a small flat screwdriver to get behind the crank. By applying pressure to the edge of the clip you can pry it from the locked position.

Fig. 9-11: Here's the same idea carried one step further. The yellow gauge carrier is accented with blue-face gauges.

Fig. 9-12: While multipiece door panels create a problem, they also give you a customizing opportunity. In this application the armrests are covered in blue against the factory gray door panels. Accents are from the trusty old red spray paint can.

(Getting it back on is an entirely different story.) Most Civics have a molded interior door handle release that is held in place by a single screw. Simply remove the screw and slide the molded piece out from around the handle. The release handle mechanism does not need to be removed.

From here the door panel is held onto the doorframe by pressure snaps. The tabs are connected to the panel and inserted into holes in the doorframe. With the panel removed, measure its width and height. Add four inches to each measurement for overlap. The overlap is vital to making the job successful.

If possible, drive the car to the fabric outlet. Take small samples or snips from the fabric rolls that appear to match. If you're trying to match vinyl or leather seats, the grain of the material as well as the color need to be taken into account. After you find a matching material, purchase enough to cover three door panels. Why three? Trust me, you'll be glad you have the extra material in reserve in the event you screw up. Even if everything goes perfectly, the extra material can be used to cover a center console or other interior components at a later date.

After you have the material, lay the door panel face down on top of the back side of the material. Fold over the sides, top and bottom. Cut a slit in the corners of the material to help ensure a wrinkle-free joint near the four corners of the panel. Next, tape one side to the back of the panel. With the material face down on a flat, smooth surface, pivot the panel to an upright position and apply a spray adhesive to the face of the panel. Carefully lower the panel back onto the material, keeping the material smooth and taunt. Turn the panel over and smooth out any wrinkles. Turn the panel back over and apply spray adhesive to the edges and fold over the material. After the adhesive has set up, take a razor blade or Exacto knife and cut x-shaped slits where the window crank and interior door handle release bay install. There you have it—a new door panel.

If you are having trouble getting the plastic tabs to snap back into place (sometimes these break from years of fatigue) you can get button screws from the fabric outlet. These clever items can be covered in the same material you used for the door panels. You simple drill new holes through the door panels and doorframes and use the button screws to secure the panels to the frame.

Another slick do-it-yourself option is to not re-cover the panels at all—instead replace them with sheet aluminum. This will give your Civic or CRX a race appearance, and the project is fairly simple and cost-

Fig. 9-13: The interior should be an extension of the exterior. Here you can see how the light blue and white paint of this Civic is matched to the blue and white vinyl found inside.

Fig. 9-14: Here's a reverse version, where a dash has been splatter-painted white with blue speckles. The seat inserts are blue; the bolsters are white.

effective. Most metal shops can cut a pair of aluminum panels to match the factory panels, which you will need to remove to use

Fig. 9-15: You can use a cage or roll bar as part of your overall interior scheme. This del Sol uses red and black leather seats with matching door panels. The three-point roll bar was painted red to integrate with the rest of the interior.

them as patterns. Have the aluminum sheet cut to match and install, using sheet metal screws or rivets. Use silver spray paint to cover the window cranks and interior door handle release bays.

Late-model Civics require a more difficult procedure than their older counterparts because these are often multipiece panels. With their shaped armrests and molded contours, late-model door panels present a greater re-covering challenge. For these panels, a good coat of vinyl paint can serve as an excellent short-term fix, but for the more visionary do-it-yourselfer these panels represent an increased opportunity for self-expression.

Gauges

Your factory gauge cluster or instrument panel is likely to be filled with the basics but short on the essentials. Sure, you need a speedometer and tachometer as well as water temperature and fuel level gauges. With the exception of higher-end trim levels, Civics and CRXs feature warning lights in the place of measured gauges for oil pressure and voltage/amperage. For most, these instruments

Fig. 9-16: A full-race Civic needs a full-race dash. The spun-aluminum panels look trick and house all the right gauges and controls. Note how the tach is mounted top and center of the gauge cluster. Also, note the knob for the on-board fire system.

are adequate, but as true performance-car geeks, we require more accurate information. What is the oil pressure measurement? Exactly how hot is the water? What's the fuel pressure? (This is very important for supercharged or turbocharged cars.) How strong is the electrical system? All this information is vital when operating a performance engine. At the very least, all these gauges will make you feel like you're driving an over-horsepowered Honda.

There are more choices for Civic gauge upgrades than for any other sport compact car. The automotive aftermarket has responded in force. You want a white gauge face? You got it. Perhaps yellow, red or blue is more to your liking? All of these colors are available. Changing the factory gauge face requires you to remove the gauge cluster from the dash. Removing the protective front plastic covering can allow you to gain access to some Civic gauges. Others will require you to remove them from behind the clear front cover.

There are several ways to mount alternative gauges. The more popular way is to place the pre-mounted gauges in clusters that attach to the driver's side inside windshield pillar. This is an excellent way to add gauges and not have to install them into less

desirable areas, such as air vents or a center console. These gauges are housed in molded carriers that either match or come very close to matching the texture and color of the factory materials.

Let us not forget the all-important tachometer. You will see many Civics with overgrown tachs the size of the original steering wheel. Let it be known that size is not important—at least when it comes to tachometers. What is important is the ability to read the gauge. The tachometer is the most vital of all your gauges. It tells you when you're in the performance band, when to shift or when you're about to launch a rod through the oil pan.

Where the tach is placed is an all-important decision. Every Honda produced with a factory tach has it placed it on the right side of the instrument panel with the speedometer on the left. This because most people are left-eye dominant. Therefore, we drive using the speedometer. However, when you are racing the tachometer reading is far more necessary than knowing the miles per hour. This is why most race car drivers prefer to have the tach dead center on the cluster. When rearranging gauges in a street car, it is preferable to switch the positions of the speedo and tach.

Fig. 9-17: A five-point cage really makes a statement, especially in a CRX. Without a back seat to get in the way, a CRX interior can be taken to the street-performance extreme. This application features a well done cover cut to fit the rearward support bars.

Shift lights have become extremely popular over the past few years—and for good reason. If I had to select one innovation that has contributed most to the advancement in Honda performance it would be the shift light. This simple device gives the driver a strobe flash indicating the optimum time to shift. Usually mounted on the extreme left side on top of the dash and facing the driver, a shift light does not require the use of an aftermarket tachometer.

Cages and Roll Bars

Roll bars and cages are designed to protect you in the event of a rollover. For 99 percent of Civic owners these safety items are thankfully never intended to be used. Aside from adding safety, a cage or roll bar stiffens the chassis as it ties points of the car together. These act like a front or rear strut brace, as described in Chapter 3.

On the surface you could say that a cage or roll bar is a waste of time, money and space. After all, if you never use your Civic in serious competition, what's the point of having a big-time safety device like a cage or bar? However, if designed, constructed and installed properly, any roll bar or cage can help improve performance.

There are several types of roll bar setups. The most basic is a simple two-point roll bar that loops from left to right, connecting to two sides of the car. Add a bar that runs from the center of the crossbar and angles down to the passenger's floorboard and a three-point bar is created. A four-point bar has angled supports that run rearward to points just below the roof support cross-members. This stiffens the car body and reduces flexing during high-speed cornering.

A "full cage" runs from the front floorboards up to the roofline to the center roll bar. The rearward bars extend to the rear cross-members. These allow for greater protection and car body rigidity.

From a simple roll bar to a full cage, each allows for the installation of racing harness belts. Be aware, though, that for day-to-day driving, the more extensive the system, the harder it is to enter and exit the car.

All the words in the world can't tell the story like seeing the real thing; thus prime examples of innovative interior designs are presented. These photos show extensive use of materials as well as the simplicity of gutting the shell to a lightweight race appearance. It's all up to you. And, unlike with paint treatments, you can change the interior over and over again without breaking the bank.

Graphically Speaking

Fig. 10-1: Here is the difference between paint and vinyl. This wild panel job is made possible by hours of work. These graphics were laid out in multiple overlays. Before spraying the candy colors, a base coat was applied. Over the candies are layers of clear. The entire job is color-sanded before being buffed to a deep finish. This is a first-class, show-winning paint job.

By this time you should be deep into your project Civic. The suspension, tires and wheels are dialed in and the engine has been upgraded to deliver more power. The clutch and shifter feel much better, as do the brakes. You've got all your body modifications completed and the interior components are in place. Now it is time to cover up all the ugly primer and factory paint that can give your ride the street-beater status.

To get to this point in your project and not give in to the temptation to apply trick paint or new-age graphics is a testament to your self-control. Many compact car enthusiasts jump in headfirst by adding graphics early on in the project, only to find that they must retouch or redo them because of damage or exposure during the construction process. It is always better to wait until you've completed as much of the construction as possible before applying custom paint or vinyl treatments.

With that said, you must now make the decision as to the style and colors that will suit your taste as well as the personality of the car. Yes, the personality of the *car*. The paint scheme you select will reveal to the world more about you and your car than any other change you will make. After you've selected a style, the biggest question has to be asked—who are you going to trust to execute this all-important change?

Custom car painters are a rare and talented breed. The best of the bunch have the ability to totally transform a Civic, CRX or del Sol from a street car to a showpiece. The average painter will, at the very least, make a street car look closer to a show car. The less skilled painter can

To look good is better than to feel good... and you look marvelous. Flames, scallops, murals, touring-style, and other visual effects.

take the same street car and turn it into a rolling mistake, so choosing a custom painter is very important.

The first step is to gather examples of paint schemes that not only catch your eye, but also stir your emotions. Don't settle with being a follower just for the sake of conformity. If you lack a sense of creativity, collecting photos from shows and events as well as what you've seen in popular magazines (inside and outside of the import performance scene) will help you develop a look that fits your car's personality.

Selecting a Style

There are millions of paint schemes that have been executed and millions more still waiting to be created. Nearly every paint scheme comes from, or is spun off of, one of the basic styles—flames, scallops, murals, panels, competition or fades.

All of the basic styles have origins in the early days of hot-rodding. Each has enjoyed and/or suffered through the evolutions over the past 40 to 50 years. Painters have applied their own touches to each style—some specialize in panels while others just do flames and scallops. Here's an overview of the basic custom paint styles.

Flames. Made popular in the 1950s on early hot rods and customs, this is a paint style that never goes out of fashion. However, Honda owners have yet to embrace the style.

Flames are generally painted in multiple contrasting colors stemming from a base or origin point usually located at the front of the vehicle. The base can be thick or thin, depending on taste. Fingers, sometimes called licks, extend from the base and follow the bodyline of the car to a tip. The individual licks can be painted to flow along the bodyline or intertwined, overlapped and woven together to create the desired effect. The base and licks are finished off with pinstriped lines that create tails. Some painters pinstripe the tips with split tails, adding to the visual motion of the flames.

There are many variations on the popular flame style, which include:

- Flame-throwers: a continuous line of small licked flames running down the side of the car.

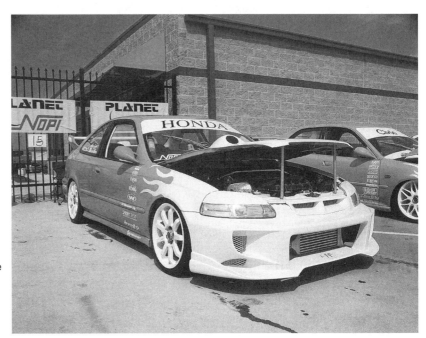

Fig. 10-2: Flames have yet to catch on; however, here is a recent flame job seen at the NOPI Nationals. Although crude and without tails, it is a step in the right direction.

Fig. 10-3: Over the years, scallops have been seen on a variety of cars and trucks. This Honda-style scallop job uses a base red with yellow reverse scallops. This is a clever and inexpensive way to create a bold statement as the door jambs, engine bay and hatchback sill did not have to be repainted.

- Ghost flames: faded flames in muted or pearl colors. These flames are rarely pinstriped. They are intended to be subtle and less dominant. Usually done in pearls, ghost flames appear and disappear depending on the angle of sight and light source.
- Flames in flames: this is when there are multiple layers of flames within themselves. Some painters have created this effect by painting one set of flames from a thick base and inserting a second set of flames from the base's front border into the first layer of flames.
- Water flames: water shapes are substituted for fire. Instead of licks, the base extensions are streams ending in oversized drops. Colors are usually limited to blue and white combinations.
- Leaf flames: unique and difficult version to apply. Here the painter uses leaf instead of paint. Leaf is a very thin material made from pressed gold or silver. The sheet is applied into the masked areas before being clear-coated.

Scallops. Also made popular in the 1950s and early '60s, scallops run in simple straight patterns with the scallop fingers decreasing in width from the base to the tip. The colors of scallops are unlimited, with the shape of the car's body generally dictating the shape of the scallops. Older Civics need more rigid lines to accommodate the sharp angles of the body. Late-model Civics can use the rounded body lines to influence the flow with angular or radius fingers.

Scallops can be applied in groups or as one design that overlaps the hood and front fenders. In the early days of customizing, painters like Watson and Roth used scallops on the hood, side, roof and trunk of massive American land yachts like Mercs, Fairlanes, Hudsons and Impalas.

Over the years scallops have gone in and out of style. Therefore, be aware that if you choose to have this style of paint applied to your New Age hot rod, you may find it to be like young love—having an intense but short life span.

Murals. This style is commonly applied as a support style to panels, scallops or fades. This is a style that not only can add person-

Fig. 10-4: If it's rolling art you're into, murals are the way to go. Checkout the Gothic details on this custom coupe. The mural spills over the hood and onto the fenders. The trunk was given a mural. The cost for a mural can range from as little as $100 for small areas to as much as $7,500 for full-scale assaults.

ality to your car but can overly personalize it as well. Large, flat sheet metal areas are tempting canvases for the airbrush artist. And, speaking of art, it is critical to carefully select an automotive muralist. A well done job can be a work of art. A poorly done mural can be a source of embarrassment.

Murals can be anything you want or anything the airbrush artist can create. From mythical warriors to tropical scenery to religious visions, the choices are endless. However, choose wisely because you are going to be forever linked with the image you select.

Some of the best examples of murals were found in the 1970s, during the height of the custom van movement, when many new auto muralists came onto the scene. This was also the time when new techniques were developed to reduce the time it takes to create rolling art. Shadow murals became

popular, with scenes depicting sailing ships, hot-air ballooning, desert activities, western ghost towns or big city skylines. Later murals became more detailed and intricate as mass production demand declined when the full-size custom van fad died.

Lowriders' murals have evolved into an art form. If it's examples of automotive art you seek, check out a few lowrider shows and you'll get a state-of-the-art eyeful.

Murals don't have to be big and bold to be effective. Small murals can accent an area, drawing attention to or away from items and components. For example, a small panel of sheet metal can be attached to the dash of a CRX or Civic and painted to fake gauges. Speaker or audio component covers can be painted into scenes to add flair to an otherwise bland box.

Here's another trick when showing your Civic: if you want the look of a performance engine but can't sink thousands of dollars in chrome and speed equipment, cut a panel of sheet metal to fit over the engine and have it painted to look like a racing Honda engine compartment. You can also use this idea on a smaller scale for radiator support covers, firewalls and trunk panels. The options are endless.

Panels. This has proven to be the most popular of all paint styles because there is no end to the variations that can be applied. From simple accents to wild overlapping schemes, anything goes. One reason panels have been so popular is that you can combine different styles into the panels. Flames look good framed within panels. The same applies to scallops and murals. However, the real power of panels is that you can select them to have no borders at all, should you wish.

Panels can be straight or can wrap, loop, fade, break or extend into door sills. Their theme can be picked up and incorporated into the interior, trunk and/or engine compartment. Some innovative Civic owners have found ways to overlay window tint to keep the theme flowing across the glass.

Fades. This style has been around for over 50 years. Some prestigious automakers as far back as 1920 started using fades to enhance the bodylines of cars. The painter takes a color and gradually blends it from dark to light or light to dark. It can also be applied to change colors for complementing hues.

A good fade job is very difficult to achieve. It takes years for a custom painter to perfect a fade technique. Fades, unlike other paint styles, don't fit every body style. Older Civics are too boxy to allow a fade to flow from front to back or top to bottom. CRX and Civic hatchback and del Sol models have good shapes for front-to-back fades. Civic coupe and sedan fades can go either front to back or top to bottom.

One key factor to keep in mind is the base color you are working from. For example, if the car is teal green, the entire body should be covered in this color. This means the door jams are teal and under the hood is teal, as are the inner-fender wells and firewall. Therefore, a good custom painter will suggest a fade that begins with a darker green on the bottom rocker panels and works its way to the roof, finishing off in a patch of lime or even frost-white. This fade will allow for the

Fig. **10-5:** This hatchback sports a cost-effective vinyl fade.

Fig. 10-6: Inspired by European and American Touring Car racing, the race look became popular in 1997. This is one of the trendy looks. More traditional racing schemes have greater longevity.

hood and fenderwells to look more natural, as the original teal is used as the overflow or mid-range color in the fade.

Starting with a Civic can be an advantage if you are doing a front-to-back fade. Use the base color as the front and fade back to the trunk. This allows you to keep the original color under the hood but will require that you repaint the door jams and trunk sill. (These areas are far easier to paint than the engine compartment.)

Fade painting has been made less popular with the advent of pre-mixed color-changing paint, such as Mystic and Spectrum. However, these paints are extremely expensive, costing as much as $5,000 to $7,000 to repaint a Civic sedan or coupe. By contrast, a fade paint job can run from $1,200 to $2,000.

Competition style. Over the past few years Competition has become the style of choice for thousands of Civic builders. The reasons for this popular style are simple: first, it is easy to do and easy to replace. Done in vinyl, many have number and sponsor logos applied to the profile of the car. The hood is reserved for a racing stripe or a major sponsor logo. While the most recent rise in popularity comes from cloning European

Touring race cars, the roots of this style date back to the early racing cars. Stripes were applied to the hoods of cars to absorb glare caused by the sun and reflecting into the eyes of the driver.

A walk through history can save you some embarrassment: when was the last time you saw a single stripe placed on the passenger's side of the hood? Knowing the original reason a hood stripe was applied, putting one on the wrong side of the hood seems pretty stupid. As time went on, manufacturers used the hood stripe as a symbol of performance, more closely linking the victories on the track with the cars in the showroom.

In the early 1960s Ford started carrying the racing stripe to the lower side-rocker panels. Within a decade every automaker used stripes to add status to their cars—nose stripes for Camaros, tail strips for Chargers, Darts and Super Bees, hockey sticks and strobe stripes for 'Cudas, and hood stripes for everyone. Today, automakers have abandoned the vinyl stripe process. Perhaps this is one reason the style has once again become more popular with enthusiasts.

New advancements in computer technology have made all these styles of graphics easier for vinyl applications. While it looks good, vinyl is never as effective as paint.

However, vinyl does give you the option of peeling off the graphics and starting over with a clean canvas.

Selecting A Painter

Finding a custom painter is not as easy as thumbing through the Yellow Pages and picking a name. Among the most famous and influential are Doug Starbuck, Pete Santini, Tom Taylor, Rob Taylor, Brian Jendro, Roly Fernandez, Phillip Vega and Kyle Gann. There are painters all across the country that can be considered master painters; however, the people mentioned have gained media recognition over the years by having their work be on the cutting edge in styling and quality.

Finding a high-quality custom painter will require you to do some research. Think outside the box and attend events for other forms of automotive customizing. Street rod events, cruise nights and lowrider shows are good places to check out the talents of area painters. Most street rodders and lowriders won't trust their cars to rookies. Therefore, these enthusiasts are good references for the painters who know their craft.

When you find two or three painters, check out the shop of each one. Ask to see their "book" of accomplishments. Measure how each reacts to your car and your ideas. The good painters will be as excited about painting your car as they would be about a rod or custom car. Also, gauge what suggestions they have for your car. If the interest is not genuine, the paint job will suffer and likely will not be completed on time. If you sense the painter is doing the job only for the money, it's best to find another painter.

The most important factor when selecting a style and a painter is the condition of the base paint. You should only proceed with custom paint if the base paint of the car is in excellent-to-mint condition. Should you have less than ideal base paint, you need to address the bigger problem before moving forward.

Whichever paint style or combination of styles you use, custom paint is a personal choice. And, while trick paint may increase the value of your Civic, CRX or del Sol, it rarely helps the ease of selling the car later in life.

Custom paint is a personal choice and needs to be viewed in that manner. In the end, it doesn't matter what everyone else is doing; it only matters what you like.

What You Can Expect to Pay

FLAMES	LOW	HIGH
Paint	$300	$1,200
Vinyl	$200	$600

SCALLOPS:	LOW	HIGH
Paint	$300	$1,200
Vinyl	$200	$600

MURALS:	LOW	HIGH
Paint	$100	$7,500
Vinyl	$100	$800

PANELS:	LOW	HIGH
Paint	$500	$3,000
Vinyl	$100	$1,500

FADES:	LOW	HIGH
Paint	$1,200	$2,000
Vinyl	$200	$1,000

COMPETITION STYLE:	LOW	HIGH
Paint	$500	$1,500
Vinyl	$200	$800

Performance Driving

Fig. 11-1: Before heading for the track, you need to put together a kit of tools that you will likely need at the event. It makes no difference if you're going straight and fast or turning left and right—a basic tool kit is necessary. A set of deep sockets, a ratchet, flat and Phillips screwdrivers, an adjustable wrench, vice grips and a small mallet should do the trick. Oh—and don't forget the tire-pressure gauge.

Here you are with your trick Civic, cruising Main Street on a Friday night. The paint is shining, the storefronts are reflected in the polished wheels, the exhaust tone echoes from the buildings. It's just you and several hundred other import performance maniacs out for a friendly get-together.

We all know where this is going to lead. Sooner or later you're going to feel the need to defend the limits of your creation. In this growing community of Honda performance drivers, your honor and driving ability are going to be questioned. When this happens (and it will), you better be ready to answer the call.

Now, not for a minute am I condoning street racing—in fact, just the opposite. Street racing is for wimps and fools. Running head to head on the street with some knucklehead is just plain stupid. You have no idea if the driver next to you has any clue how to drive. You don't know if the other car is safe. There is no formal staging, starting and timing equipment, and the pavement may not be suitable for racing. In other words, real performance enthusiasts take it to the track.

Taking your Civic to the track requires you (and others) to play by a specific set of rules. All cars must first pass a safety inspection, helping to protect you, the other participants and the spectators. You run in classes dictated by your ability and experience as well as by the modifications made to your car.

Over the past few years, import drag racing has become the rage. One of the basic reasons drag racing has become so popular is that it takes far less time and skill to achieve results. However, the design and drive-

Making your Civic fast is one thing, handling the power is another. Here are the basics in learning how to corner, brake and drag race.

line configuration of Civics, del Sols and CRXs are better suited for SCCA (Sports Car Club of America) Solo and road racing.

Each weekend there are a large number of motorsports events throughout the world. Many are broadcast live or telecast on tape to millions of enthusiasts. The venue may be NASCAR, Formula 1, Indy Car, CART, SCCA or drag racing. Whatever the form of motorsports, we can all marvel and admire the skill of the drivers involved.

As we watch from the grandstands or from the comfort of our living rooms, each of us would gladly give up our vantagepoint for the one behind the steering wheel.

Piloting a NASCAR-prepared stockcar at 200 miles per hour takes skill, concentration and confidence. Likewise, guiding a powerful race-built NSX through the twists and turns of Laguna Seca or Watkins Glen also takes an acquired skill. As you watch the action, you can imagine yourself rocketing down the front straight with the roar of the crowd reverberating through the car. As impossible as taking part in major racing events might seem, it is quite easy to get involved in motorsports activities in or near your hometown.

There are two basic forms of sportsman style racing. One is solo and the other is drag racing. Each has its own sponsoring or sanctioning bodies. In solo racing, SCCA has prepared the rules and basic foundation for participation. In drag racing there are a number of organizations that have come into existence, including NIRA (National Import Racing Association), IDRC (Import Drag Racing Circuit) and NHRA (National Hot Rod Association).

Road Racing/Autocross

While drag racing has become popular, solo-style (also known as autocross) racing is better suited for your Honda product—and a lot more fun to participate in. The SCCA has organized many racing programs designed to get you started in motorsports. For a small entry fee (usually under $25), you can drive your Civic, CRX or del Sol under real racing conditions without the risk of wheel-to-wheel contact. Each weekend dozens of cities host this type of SCCA Solo racing events.

In addition to having a great place to test the performance of your Honda, this form of racing requires little or no experience to get started. Autocross competitions are ideal for beginning your racing interest, even if you've never pushed your car to the limit.

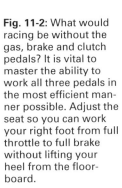

Fig. 11-2: What would racing be without the gas, brake and clutch pedals? It is vital to master the ability to work all three pedals in the most efficient manner possible. Adjust the seat so you can work your right foot from full throttle to full brake without lifting your heel from the floorboard.

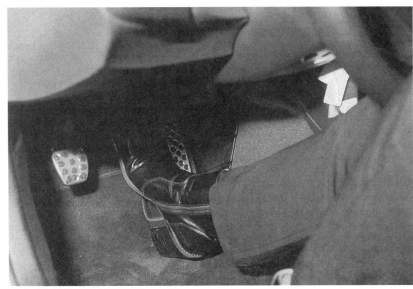

Fig. 11-3: Unlike the drag strip racing, autocross events travel from location to location. Therefore, the timing and "central control" area is likely to be a mobile home or specially equipped trailer. But make no mistake, these are sophisticated racing information centers specially designed for accuracy.

Fig. 11-4: Position your hands at nine and three o'clock. Your arms should be slightly bent.

Autocross events help you become a better driver, both on the track and during everyday commuting. The better you know the limitations of your driving skills and your car, the greater your chance of avoiding trouble when demanding conditions present themselves.

Using the skills you develop on the track can translate into more enjoyable daily dri-

Fig. 11-5: You should be able to turn the steering wheel 180 degrees to the right and left without taking your hands off the wheel. Likewise, your elbows should not be able to touch your chest.

ving. That sweeping on-ramp you use everyday can now become an apex practice drive. Every winding road turns into an opportunity for understanding weight transfer. While day-to-day travel is generally uneventful, using the same skills and techniques practiced on the track make your Civic more fun during low-speed driving.

The first important piece of knowledge is basic seat positioning. The ability to effectively reach the steering wheel, and shift knob and correctly operate the foot pedals is vital. Start by adjusting the seat so your right leg is slightly bent and you can pivot your right foot from full throttle to zero throttle and over to full brake without removing your heel from the floorboard.

Next, adjust your seat-back position by holding the steering wheel at three o'clock and nine o'clock. Turn the wheel 180 degrees in both directions, crossing your arms without removing your hands from the wheel. If your elbows touch your chest your seat is too close. If your hands must leave the steering wheel, your seat is too far back.

The gearshift knob should be within easy reach. You should be able to shift through the gears without leaning forward. This simple seating guideline will enable you to make precise steering and gear changes

with minimal effort. Precision shifting and steering make for improved control. More control is rewarded with smoother, more consistent driving. Smooth and consistent driving performance is what professional race car drivers strive to accomplish.

The second step to smoother driving is hand position. It is common during daily driving to have the left hand on the steering wheel and the right on the gearshift knob. While this looks like a cool position, it is not a preferred technique for performance driving. The best place for both your hands is on the steering wheel. After executing a gear change, return your right hand to the three o'clock position. This is a good habit to develop during your everyday commutes. In addition to the benefit of better steering-wheel control, the movement of the right hand from the steering wheel to the shifter also promotes better shifting technique. But more on that later.

By having the driver's seat in the correct position and both hands on the steering wheel as much as possible, you improve your feel for the car. "Feel" is that magical quality that can make a good driver a great one. When you're seated correctly and you let your hands feel the car, it provides you with more complete information as the car trans-

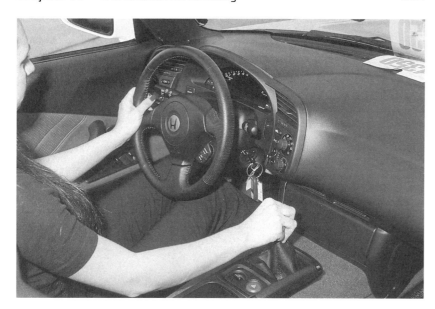

Fig. 11-6: Shifting through the gears is quicker when you flick the wrist and forearm rather than pushing and pulling the entire arm.

fers weight during cornering and braking. Feeling a Civic's weight transfer allows you a better understanding of the car's limits.

Exploring the performance edge of your Civic, CRX or del Sol is what justifies all the upgrades in the suspension, tires, wheels and engine. At no time in history has the opportunity for all-out Honda performance been more perfectly timed. To have all the tools to make your car faster and handle better and not be willing to test the boundaries is a waste of time and machinery. All of this exploration starts with seat and hand positioning to achieve a better feel.

When you master the feel of your Civic, you'll find that your confidence will skyrocket. If you begin to push your Civic before understanding its limits and yours, you will likely end up in the rotary club. In other words, the rear tires and wheels will be coming around to meet the fronts.

Weight transfer is the simple part of the feel process and plays an important role in achieving proper cornering control. However, as easy as it is, this is also the most misunderstood part as well. When you accelerate, weight is shifted from the front of the car to the back. Under braking, the weight shifts from back to front. The movement is like waves coming ashore and then receding into

the ocean. Weight transfer under acceleration and braking is easy to control while operating in a straight line. The weight shifts to

Fig. 11-7: After successfully completing each gear change, return your right hand to its position on the steering wheel.

Fig. 11-8: Correctly transferring the weight of the car is a vital formula to autocross success.

the rear when you press the gas. As you level the acceleration, the energy caused during the weight transfer slowly evens out and the Civic gets closer to a neutral weight position. Hitting the brakes transfers the energy forward, causing the front of the car to dip. This energy also levels as braking is eased.

We have all felt and dealt with simple weight transfer. Now add a left or right turn into the formula. Everything changes as the weight and energy find a home in the flow of the energy. A left-hand turn under acceleration sends massive force to the right rear of the car. Likewise, braking while performing a right-hand turn lifts all the weight from the left rear of the car. With all this going on at one time, you must control the transfer of weight by either lifting off the gas and applying the brakes or pulling off the brakes and accelerating out of the turn. It sounds complicated and intimidating, but it all comes down to finessing the feel.

An easy way to experience weight transfer is to enter a sweeping highway on-ramp at a safe speed. Stay as far outside the turn as possible and accelerate slightly around the turn. Keeping a wide apex as you approach the end of the turn, lift off the gas and the car will turn toward the inside of the turn. You'll feel the transfer of weight from the rear of the car to the front. When you accelerate out of the turn, you'll transfer weight back to the rear wheels as you enter the highway and the flow of traffic.

Okay, stop scratching your head because you don't understand how to discover the apex of a turn. To find the apex, you must first understand that every turn has four basic components. The "brake-in" point is the first element in a turn, the spot where braking begins. The "turn-in" point is where you enter a turn. Next comes the "apex" or the innermost point of the turn. Finally, there is the "track-out" spot where you will

Fig. 11-9: At the turn-in point the steering wheel should be wound and unwound smoothly, as you brake into and accelerate out of the turn.

unwind the steering wheel and drift to the outside of the turn while accelerating.

Don't expect to be a master of the apex right away. In fact, most professional race car drivers will tell you that you will never be a perfect cornering king—nobody is. Getting good at the technique takes time, practice and discipline. Here are a few key tips:

- When approaching the brake-in point, squeeze the brake pedal gently and evenly.
- Visually pick out the apex of the turn.
- Smoothly turn the wheel from the turn-in point to the apex.
- Don't turn too soon. A common trick is to not turn the steering

Fig. 11-10: Clipping the apex of the turn is the goal. If you turn too late you will not be able to take full advantage of the turn and will have to back off on the power.

wheel until just before you can see the track-out through the apex of the turn.

- Point the car at the apex, lift off the brake and accelerate while unwinding the steering wheel.
- Drift to the track-out point and onto the next corner or straightaway.

How do you know if you're working a corner correctly? You can get your answer by checking the following:

- If your wheels are locking up, you're jabbing the brakes. Braking too late or misjudging the severity of the turn usually causes this.
- If you're coasting into a turn, you are applying the brakes too soon, thus losing valuable momentum. This will also result in improper weight transfer.
- If you have to turn the steering wheel in the direction of the turn more than once, this indicates that you're starting your turn too soon and likely are passing the apex.
- If you can't fully accelerate at the apex, you've missed it due to turning too late.

When you hit the turn correctly, the entire process will feel smooth and you will feel in control. You will be able to downshift or brake smoothly at the brake-in point, point your car at the apex under acceleration and unwind the steering wheel and drift to the edge of the track-out.

The straightaways need to be attacked as aggressively as the turns. This is the fun zone—a place to put the hammer down. This is also the setup area. Good drivers use the straightaways to set up the next series of turns.

Hitting the maximum speed of your Civic in the straightaways is important and hitting the track-out points in turns is even more important. A straightaway needs to be approached from the track-out point and picking a line that will prepare you for the brake-in point of the next turn.

This brings us to the fun part of driving: shifting. Running through the gates. Speed shifting. Banging off the gears. Pounding the teeth. However you put it, precise, effective shifting of gears is a revered art.

Gear changes are quicker and more effective when made with a flick of the wrist instead of a long throw of the arm. You need to relate the distance traveled by your arm to the distance traveled by the shifter. You installed a short-throw shifter to cut down on the time and distance needed to transfer from gear to gear. This same theory applies to the movement of your hand and arm.

Nature supplied your arm with an elbow, a wonderful joint that can make shifting quicker. Allow your elbow to be the pivot point of your shifting, moving your arm fore and aft in quick, short bursts.

Hand position on the shift knob is important for fast, positive shifting. There are two basic methods for handling the shifter knob. The first method is to cover the knob by placing its top in the palm of your hand. Your fingertips are relaxed and pointed down. You will use the folds of your fingers (from the inside middle joints to the area where your fingers and palm meet) to shift from 1-2 gear, 3-4 gear on the upshifts and 5-4 and 3-2 gear during downshifts. Shifting from 2-3 and 4-5 will be done with the force coming from the lower palm (that is, where the hand connects to the wrist).

The other method is to grip the knob like a pistol. The knob is cradled in the palm of the hand with the thumb and index fingers wrapped around the head of the shift knob. The same set of joints and muscles are used as in the first method; the difference is the angle of the wrist. I find the second method reduces the possibility of fatigue in the forearm.

Working the clutch and shifter in unison takes a great deal of practice. First you must set your Civic clutch where you like it. Some drivers like to ride the clutch pedal. If you do this, you will want your Civic's clutch to engage at the bottom of the pedal travel. Others like the pedal to be responsive closer to the top. This allows for a tap of the pedal to engage the clutch. This may seem better, and in most competition cases it is. However, if you are in the habit of keeping your foot on the pedal, you'll be installing a number of clutches in a short period of time.

Speed-shifting through the gears is needed to keep the rpm levels at or near the peak torque range. The secret is not to only master the technique but also to know the optimum performance range of your drivetrain. For example, if your Civic's performance range is above 3,500 rpm, this becomes the green line on the tachometer. In other words, you don't want the engine to fall under this rpm range. This is vastly different from drag racing. Autocross and roadracing requires you to watch more than just a shiftstrobe. You live, drive and die by the tachometer. Good shifting techniques and knowledge will keep you in the hunt.

So, how do you speed-shift? This is a timing game between your left foot and your right hand. As you depress the clutch you throw the shifter into the next gear. From a standing start, pushing the pedal to the floor and jamming the shifter back into second gear is fairly easy to do. Doing the same from

second to third is a different matter altogether. There's a little speed bump called a gate that you must also negotiate. Once you get to third, shifting into forth is a snap.

Okay, fine; you've made it up through the gears, but here comes a corner. Now you must run down through the gears and still keep the engine in the powerband or use the rpm range to save the brakes. Being able to shift quickly down the gears is where you separate the contenders from the pretenders.

The best way to perfect your shifting technique is by running the gears dry—that is, by sitting in your car and shifting over and over again while the engine is off. This is no different from Tiger Wood on the driving range or Tony Gwynn hitting off the batting tee. It's all about mind and muscle memory. When you get out onto the track, your head, feet and arms will have a better chance of working together.

One of the best aspects of autocross racing is that the track layout is going to be different for every event. The layout depends on the event master or coordinator. If a Corvette club sponsors the event, the track will likely be wider and will feature sweeping turns and longer straightaways to help use the V8 power. If a Porsche club runs the event, you may have tighter turns with shorter straights.

Fig. 11-11: Having a safe haven can help save both you and your equipment from the elements.

Fig. 11-12: Protecting your head is not only important—it's required.

Knowing in advance who is running the event may help you better prepare your Civic prior to the event.

When you arrive at an event, you first establish your pit area. The pits are usually unreserved and wide open—first come, first serve. Once you've got your pit area marked, unload your support items, including tools and extra components (spark plugs, wires, lugnuts, fluids, jack and jackstands, ramps, creeper, special tires and wheels, coolers, chairs, etc.). Some veteran racers bring an easy-up-style tent or covering to keep them and their cars protected from the elements (sun, rain or fog). Racing may require you to have a support crew. This will make competing more fun. When you participate at an event with a group of friends, you can all share in the excitement and help support each other with both parts and encouragement.

The next step is to go through tech and spec. This procedure gets your car inspected and approved for the event. What the offi-cials are looking for is to ensure that the proper safety devices are in place and all the vital components (brakes, exhaust, throttle returns, safety equipment, helmet, etc.) are working correctly.

This also is the time you and your car will be put into a class and run group. A vehicle and driver class is determined by the modi-fications made to the car and the experience level of the driver. There is everything from showroom stock to full-race modified class-es, with novice to pro driver classifications.

For autocross events, there are two basic setups. The first is a solo course, where you race against the clock. Cones mark the course. The object is to navigate through the course staying within the cones. Knocking down or moving a cone from its position results in a time-added penalty.

Cars and drivers are put into run groups. When your run group is called, you head for the staging area. Most events provide for a chance to walk the course before the event or at the lunch break. This is a very important part of the event because walking the course allows you to mentally prepare for your run. As you sit in the staging area, you can mentally go through the turns, planning your brake-in and power-out points. Rather than driving to the staging area, it is advisable to use your friends as a crew to push the car there in order to keep the temperature in the engine com-partment down as well as to keep the brakes cool. As you get within a few cars of the start-ing line, start the engine, put on your gloves and helmet and latch the harness or seatbelts.

As you reach the starting line, you will be started either by a yellow to green light or by a flagman. Either way, your time will not begin until your front wheel trips the timing beam. Continue your run until you com-plete the course and trip the timing beam at the finish line. The only thing that should prevent you from completing the run is if a course worker presents a yellow or red flag.

At the end of the run you will be handed a time slip showing your elapsed time for that run plus any penalties (for leaving the track or dislodging a cone). If you leave the track, miss a turn or fail to complete the course, you will receive a DNF (did not finish) status. A DNF counts as an official run. Depending on the size of the event, you will be given three to five official runs. There are also practice runs prior to your run group. Between the practice and run groups, you should be able to get in quite a bit of track time.

The second style of SCCA solo racing is Solo II. This is exactly like regular autocross events—only different. The difference is that there are two courses set up side by side. The two mirror each other, beginning with a drag-race-style start. At the end of the opening straight, one lane turns to the right while the other turns to the left. The courses are the same length with the same turns in the same places. The courses end in another set of straights leading to the final timing traps.

There are trade-off advantages to having either an early or late run group. Early run groups may benefit from cooler, denser air, which will provide better usable horsepower, especially for Honda engines. Later run groups get more rubber on the course and warmer surfaces, which can provide better traction. This is why most events run the smaller engine displacement and horsepower groups (which includes Honda Civics) earlier in the event and save the maximum traction possibilities of the late run groups for the Corvettes, Cobras and higher-horsepower competition cars.

As the heat of the day and track change, you will need to make adjustments in cam timing, air/fuel mixture and tire air pressure. This is what these events are all about—adapting and adjusting to conditions to get the most from your car. The more you participate in autocross events, the better you will get to know and expand the limits of your Civic and your personal driving skills.

Fig. 11-13: While in the staging lane, mentally prepare yourself for the task ahead. You should have already walked the course and have some idea of how you need to approach each turn and straightaway.

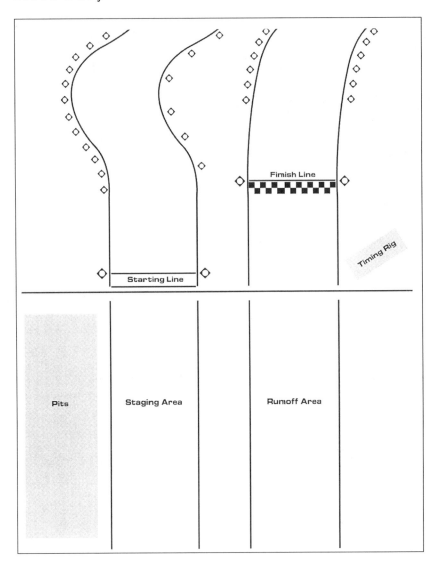

Fig. 11-14: Autocross courses are different for every event. However, the basic steps before and after each run remain the same.

Drag Racing

It's all the rage—the two-lane blacktop just 1,320 feet from staging lights to finish line. Running flat out for 9 to 19 seconds. This is the quick adrenaline rush of motorsports. It looks simple: pull up to the line, mash the gas when the light turns green and keep your foot to the floor until you cross the finish line. A piece of cake. A walk in the park.

The reality is that there is a little bit more to it than just grab and go. Like all forms of racing, drag racing takes practice. This is why local law enforcement has problems with street racing. Every straight piece of pavement can be turned into a makeshift

drag strip. The downside to this is that street racing rarely builds upon the skills needed to be successful on the real track.

Drag racing is as much psychological as it is physical. Mentally preparing yourself for an ideal run and putting a head-trip on your opponents takes special training that can't be found on the street. Getting to know the lay of drag race land and the pitfalls to avoid normally takes many sessions to discover. To give you a jump start into the world of drag racing, here are the basics.

First, it is important to know that it is often the performance of the driver, not the car, that determines the first one to reach the end of the track. To perform at your peak, it

Fig. 11-15: The Christmas Tree is the unique starting device used in drag racing. The top yellow lamps indicate you are pre-staged. The yellow lamps directly below them show you have become staged and are ready for the countdown. The tree lights run from top to bottom with three amber lamps until the green light glows. The red light at the bottom is the lamp you don't want to light up. This indicates you have left the line too soon and are disqualified.

is vital to keep your emotions in check; you must enter into the event with a cool head. Try to keep from letting the little things upset you. Even if you can't get your Civic dialed in as well as you want, you need to compensate for it with driving skill.

Drag racing requires extreme mental concentration, especially at the starting line. At this point you need to be completely focused on getting off the line with the lowest possible reaction time.

Before you can have a good reaction time, you need to know how the staging, timing and starting lights work. The "Christmas Tree" is the information and starting device used in all organized drag racing events. At the top are lights that display pre-staged and staged status. These are measured as the front wheels break the light beam near the starting line. Once you trip the pre-stage light, roll very slowly toward the starting line to bring your car to the staged status. This is where some competitors play mind games. They may want you to stage before they do. Many drivers believe that this gives them the edge as the time between staging and yellow-to-go is short.

Once both cars are staged, the starter allows the lights to run from yellow to green. In a "pro-start" process, all the yellows light

Fig. 11-16: Move up to the line slowly to engage the pre-stage lights. It is only a few inches before you are fully staged, so be sure you're ready to go before becoming fully staged.

Fig. 11-17: When the lights go from amber to green, it's time to get the heck out of Dodge City. Timing lights are set up at the 60-foot, 660-foot and finish line.

at once, followed by the green. Getting off the line too soon is called "red lighting," and a racer who jumps is disqualified from the race.

The green light does NOT start the timing process: it is when your front wheels roll off the line that the clock starts. This why you can have a quicker elapse time and still lose a race. Remember, it's still about who gets to the finish line first.

But what is reaction time? Reaction time is the measurement of the fraction of a second it takes to launch the front wheels through the staging beams after the "Christmas Tree" turns from yellow to green. There are two basic factors that can determine reaction time—the driver and the vehicle's performance. For you, the driver, reaction time is the amount of time it takes for you to recognize the changing of the lights from yellow to green and to release the clutch and press the gas. Vehicle reaction time is how long it takes for the car to react to your commands. This is where the entire car needs to be in harmony—the clutch, transmission, engine, tires, body rigidity. In short, everything must be working together to achieve the optimum launch.

The best way to improve reaction time is to participate in 1/8-mile drag racing events. These events promote shorter runs but require all the same basic skills needed for 1/4-mile tracks. Generally, 1/8-mile events allow you to have more runs, as the length of each run is shorter. You may be able to get in as many as 20 runs in a day as opposed to maybe 10 runs at a 1/4-mile practice day. When you're not on the track, watch other racers. Visualize yourself on the line and react as if you really are. This reinforces the muscle memory needed to connect mind and body.

Improving the reaction time of your Civic can be accomplished by increasing the traction factor. Tires and springs play a major role in gaining an advantage through traction. Revisit the techniques highlighted in Chapter 3. Another way to improve reaction time is by weight. Some cars react better by having weight added to help push the drive wheels to the ground. Other cars hook up without extra weight and thus get rolling quicker with less weight to pull from a standing start.

To get better traction, spend a few seconds in the burnout box, an area designed

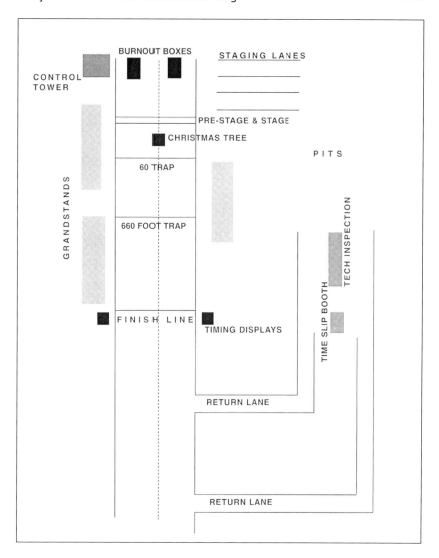

to allow you to heat up your tires and knock loose any collected debris. This is the time to heat up the tires, not to impress your friends with how well you can smoke your tires. For harder-compound street tires, a few spins will do the trick. Stay out of the waterbox when you run street tires. Treaded tires do not benefit from the waterbox. In fact, trying to use water on street tires only spreads the water out on the staging areas. This bonehead move will make you an unpopular participant for the rest of the event. If you're running on slicks (which means you should be way beyond this section of the book), 4 to 5 seconds of wheel-spinning while holding a stationary position

will be adequate. This is usually done with the assistance of water. Unlike the spectacular burnouts you see pro racers of the NHRA make where they smoke the tires to the 60-foot markers, in street classes, if you pass the starting line while attempting a burnout, you can be disqualified.

Finally, you're up to the line. You've staged in your Civic and slowly rolled up to final staging. The amber lights count down to green, and you launch. The first set of timing lights you pass through are at 60 feet. This is a very important measurement, as it will indicate how consistent your Civic is in leaving the line. Most street Civics will cover the first 60 feet in about 2 to 2.5 seconds. By way of contrast, an NHRA Top Fuel dragster can do it in about 0.600 seconds.

Halfway down the 1/4-mile track is the 660-foot line. At this point your ET is measured again. This is a good way to judge your shifting skills, as you should be in or about to shift into fourth gear. From here to the final traps it is all about standing on the gas.

At last you reach the finish line (anywhere from 10 to 20 seconds from leaving the Christmas Tree). As your Civic's front wheels break the final set of timing light beams, your elapsed time and top speed are locked in.

The 1/4 mile track is backed up with another 1/4 mile of shutdown or slowdown area. Beyond that, most tracks feature yet another 1/8 mile of emergency shutdown track, followed by the panic sandpit, which is designed to do two things: stop your car and screw up your paint job. Rarely, if ever, will you need to use the sandpit.

Within the slowdown area are turnouts that lead back to the pit area. Most tracks offer at least two turnouts. After your run, and during the slowdown, you can use any of the turnouts you feel comfortable with. They will all lead to the same place, the return road to the pits.

As you head back to the pit area along the return road, you will get your time slip. This is a vital part of the sport because it allows you to evaluate your performance—as both as a driver and a car builder. Tracks usually feature an area for distribution of the time slips. Larger tracks have a time-slip booth along the return road. Other tracks hand out the time slip at the tower. A time slip will tell you your reaction time, 60-foot time, 660-foot (1/8-mile) time, elapsed time for the full run, and top speed.

It is important to realize that the thrill of racing, be it autocross or drag racing, also comes with risks. Every time you run your Civic, CRX or del Sol at an event, you must face the possibility of bringing it home on a flatbed truck or trailer. The likelihood of mechanical breakdown is intensified during the extremely demanding conditions

brought on in motorsports activities. While you may have built your Civic with great care and expense, pushing it to the limit requires you to spend extra attention on detail so as not to overextend the tolerances of each component. However, you have an advantage over other car owners/tuners. You've got a Honda product—and in this world, that makes all the difference.

Driving Schools

Bob Bondurant School of High Performance Driving
www.bondurant.com

Frank Hawley Drag Racing School
888.901.7223

Skip Barber Racing School
www.skipbarber.com

Derek Daly Academy
800.463.3735
www.derekdaly.com

Mid-Ohio School
614.793.4615
www.midohioschool.com

Panoz Racing School
800.849.7223
www.roadatlanta.com

Jim Russell Racing Drivers School
707.939.7600
www.russellracing.com

Richard Petty Driving Experience
Drivetech
562.806.0306
www.drivetech.com

Getting Involved

Fig.12-1: A good club can be your lifeline to optimizing the enjoyment of your Civic, CRX or del Sol. Whether at the drag strip, an autocross event or show, attending and participating with fellow club members adds to the fun and overall experience.

H ere you are with your Civic, CRX or del Sol tricked out and all ready for play. What you need now is someplace to go and some other Honda enthusiasts to go with. Perhaps there is no better way to maximize the thrill and excitement of building and getting active with your entry-level Honda than in a club.

If you're in an area where there are more than five Hondas, no doubt there is some sort of enthusiasts' club. It is now your Civic duty to seek out these otherwise-demented people and join up with them to intensify your pocket rocket blitz.

Getting involved in a club can offer a perfect blend of camaraderie and education. It is a social set of people who travel in fast circles. It is also a vital ingredient in the overall pleasure of owning a performance Honda.

In simple terms, a club is designed to bring together people with a common interest or goal. For Civic owners, this is the advancement of compact car performance. Civic, CRX and del Sol owners have become the foundation for a handful of national clubs and the staple vehicle for hundreds of regional groups.

As recently as 10 years ago, there were only a few clubs specially dedicated to Honda owners. It wasn't until the advent of *Sport Compact Car* magazine that small-engine-powered cars started to become accepted. By 1994 the wheels were in motion, as dozens of regional clubs had started up. During this remarkable growth period nearly all regional clubs were all-inclusive. It didn't matter if you had a Civic, Ford Escort, Nissan Sentra or Toyota Celica. As long as owners were into compact car

It's more fun to be in the pack than a lone wolf. Here's what you need to know before you join.

customizing, all were welcome. As interest grew, some clubs were created to cater strictly to Honda owners. Today, clubs such as East Coast Hondas claim hundreds of members in several states.

On a national level, there are several associations where Civic owners can find benefits in membership. The oldest and most established is the SCCA. This large organization is responsible for the majority of autocross and sportsman road racing events in the USA. If you are into racing, the SCCA can offer you the benefits of discounts on event participation and ongoing updates on rules and classification information. By attending local chapter meetings and through participation in autocross events, your performance driving skills and knowledge of how to better your Honda are accelerated. The SCCA is an outstanding organization that has been around for decades. However, you should be aware that anyone who owns a car of any make and model can join.

Over the years the SCCA has not done a good job at creating a welcoming atmosphere for Honda racers. The average age of SCCA members is closer to Grecian Formula users than that of GAP shoppers. Recently, the upper brass of the SCCA has finally realized that the future of its grassroots efforts will fail if they don't pay attention to Honda enthusiasts.

In 1998, the Honda-Acura Club (HAC) launched its program aimed directly and solely for Honda and Acura performance enthusiasts. During the first year of operation, close to 8,000 members signed on. The model for the Honda-Acura Club is the Miata Club of America (MCA). By way of contrast, the MCA grew to 30,000 members in just three years with a high level of acceptance. The HAC has yet to attain this pace. Also, as of yet, local chapters have not been established, and all the major benefits have yet to be put into place. However, it is a start. Only time will tell if the HAC will catch on.

The Super Street Power Club (SSPC) was launched in early 2000. With the backing of the magazine of the same title and emap usa, the SSPC is designed to bring the same level of success as the model for the club, the Hot Rod Power Club. The major reason for joining the SSPC is the large number of product discounts and rebates offered by leading aftermarket manufacturers.

Enough about big, national clubs—let's talk about local clubs, the real heart and soul of mass participation for Honda Civic enthusiasts. Locating a local club is usually a hit-or-miss situation, because most local clubs are not well-organized or tightly run. Therefore, you will need to be in the right place at the right time in order to approach or be approached by some clubs.

If you are more proactive than reactive, there are ways to seek out clubs within your area. One way is to check local tuner shops and ask the shop owners what the best clubs are in the area. A second way is to attend events. This is a good way not only to find clubs but also to check out the behavior of the club members at the same time. Most serious Honda performance enthusiasts want to distance themselves from goofs and jerks. While you can never avoid knuckleheads altogether, reducing exposure will make your club experience much more satisfying.

Most local clubs start out as a group of friends who have centered their lifestyle around the building of their cars. This works just fine until the club grows to include enthusiasts outside the original group. It is at this time that the fun starts to become work. Because the house is built on a shaky foundation, it soon begins to fall apart.

When selecting a club, check out two or three meetings before becoming a card-carrying member. Attend an event as a non-member to observe the club members in action. See how well the club interacts with other clubs as well as the members among themselves. If all checks out, go to phase two.

Phase two will be to ask to see the club's bylaws. Any well-formed and well-run club will operate with a code of conduct set forth in the bylaws. Once you're comfortable with carrying the club's logo on your Civic, it's time to commit and become a member.

So, you've set your standards and none of the local clubs share your views. This may require that you start your own club. The best way to get your club together is to go to local street rod and muscle car club meetings. On the surface, this may sound a bit strange. However, these clubs have been around much longer than compact car clubs. Going to these meetings may show you things you want to incorporate into your club. It will likely also expose you to a dose of car club politics. The key is to absorb everything, extract the better elements and discard (but don't forget) the useless parts.

Getting the word out on the streets will involve being smart and organized. First, design club flyers to disperse to potential members. Get to know speed shop and tuner shop owners and workers: they can be valuable in directing members to you. Go to events—a lot of events. The more your club's name and logo get out there, the better known the club will become.

Set up a strong set of club bylaws. While this may deter some car owners from becoming involved, it will bring your club respect and ultimately attract the cream of the Honda enthusiasts.

Next, you will need a good, centrally located meeting place. Be sure to select a place that has plenty of parking. If you set up your club in a proper fashion, growth will come quickly. Therefore, you're going to need the space.

The most important factor in running a club is to be inclusive. It is a mistake to judge potential members by the quality of the Hondas they drive. It is more important to have quality members than just having Hondas that look good at shows or turn fast times at the track. Set up the meetings and events to include the input of all the members, not just the officers.

In order to have the club grow in numbers and status, strive to be involved in events outside the normal compact car cir-

cles. To do this, may require you to convince other local car clubs that your club is different from other import performance clubs. For the most part, street rodders and muscle car clubs don't like mixing with mini-truckers or import performance car owners. This is because we have not always behaved responsibly at multi-interests events. It is hard for the elders of the car club world to recognize that we are no different from the way they were 30 or 40 years ago.

The club you decide to join or run, be it existing or new, is your fingerprint on the Honda world. Choose wisely and act responsibly. The automotive world has woken up to the fact that import performance (especially Honda) is their future. Banding together greatly helps the cause. Well-run, solid clubs provide even greater emphasis to the message—it's time to recognize us, because we are here to stay.

National Clubs

SCCA (Sports Car Club of America)
9033 E. Easter Place,
Englewood, CO 80112
Phone: (303) 694-7222
Fax: (303) 694-7391
www.scca.org

Honda Acura Club
P.O. Box 11882
Marina Del Rey, CA 90295
(310) 822-6163
www.hondaclub.com

Super Street Power Club
5764 Pacific Center Blvd. Ste. 108
San Diego, CA 92121
(858) 643-9324
www.superstreetclub.com

Resources

A&A
909.974.1120
www.a-aspec.com

Advanced Engine Management, Inc. (AEM)
www.aempower.com
John Concialdi
Kirk Miller

Alamo Motorsports
210.637.0373
www.alamosports.com

American Honda
310.783.3170
www.honda.com

American Racing Wheels
310.537.0820
Tracy Robinson
www.americanracing.com

Arias Pistons
310.532.9737
www.ariaspistons.com

ARP
805.278.7223

Auto Meter
815.895.8141
www.autometer.com

Autobuzz
323.932.6210
www.autobuzz.com
Coy Gupta

AXZ Tuning
516.599.7046
www.axztuning.com

B&M
818.882.6422
www.bmracing.com

BBK
909.735.2400

Bell Engineering
210.349.6515
www.bellengineering.net
Corky Bell

Bob Bondurant Driving School
520.796.1111
www.bondurant.com
Bob Bondurant

BFGoodrich Tires
864.458.4737
Lowell Eckart

Carrillo Rods
949.498.1800
www.carrilloind.com

Chop Shop
760.480.7435
Brian Jendro

Classic Soft Trim
559.499.6888
Dennis Patterson

Clutch Master
909.877.6800
www.clutchmasters.com
Chris Jewell

Cooltech Brakes
310.219.2888
Jeff Hays

Cone Engineering
714.828.3580
www.coneeng.com

Crane Cams
904.252.1151

Crower Cams
619.422.1191
www.crower.com

Cunningham Rods
310.538.0605
www.cunninghamrods.com

DC Sports
909.734.2030
www.dcsports.com

Derek Daly Academy
702.643.2126
www.derekdaly.com
Derek Daily

DPR
310.328.9488
www.dpr-racing.com

Drivetech
562.806.0306
www.drivetech.com

DSCG, Inc.
619.463.5100
Brad Trimmer

Electromotive
703.331.0100
www.electromotive-inc.com

Ed Hanson Exhaust Systems
619.698.7030
Ed Hanson

Eibach Springs
949.752.6700
www.eibach.com
Gary Peek

Exedy
734.454.0600

FMAX
760.746.6638
www.f-max.com

Frank Hawley Drag Racing School
909.622.2466
Frank Hawley

Greddy Performance
949.588.8300
www.greddy.com

Hahn Racecraft
630.801.1417
www.hahnrace.com

H&R Springs
360.738.8881
Roland Graef

HKS
310.763.9600

Honda/Acura Club
310.822.0080
www.hondaclub.com
Jeff Donker

Hyperco Springs
219.722.8230
Kelly Falls
Pat Sofie

IDRC
714.536.8029
www.importdrag.com

Ingalls
303.651.1297
www.ingallseng.com

Intrax Springs
714.252.0800
www.intraxsuspension.com

Jackson Racing
888.888.4079
www.jacksonracing.com
Oscar Jackson

Jacobs Electronics
915.685.3345
www.jacobselectronics.com
Dr. Christopher Jacobs

Jet Performance
714.848.5515
www.jetchip.com

JG Engine Dynamics, Inc.
431 S. Raymond Ave., #102
Alhambra, CA 91803
626.281.5326
Javier Gutierrez

Jim Russell Racing School
800.773.0345
www.russellracing.com

JM Motorsports
858.689.1124
Lawrence Prijoles

JUN
562.424.7828
www.junusa.com

K&N Engineering
909.684.9762
Nate Shelton

Koni
606.586.4100

Knight Engineering
661.940.1215
www.ice-man.com

Lowrider Magazine
909.598.2300

Mid-Ohio School
614.793.4600

Modern Image
714.375.0591

Momo
949.380.7556

MTX Speakers
608.328.2552

Neuspeed
805.388.8111
www.neuspeed.com
Greg Woo

NHRA
626.914.4761
www.nhra.com

NIRA
323.782.2610
Craig Lieberman

Nitrous Express
940.767.7694
www.nitrousexpress.com

Nitrous Works
706.864.7009

Nology
760.591.0888
www.nology.com
Werner Funk

NOPI
404.366.4700
www.nopi.com
Mike Meyers

NOS
714.545.0580
www.nosnitrous.com

PaceSetter Exhaust
602.233.1818
Fred Gerle

Panoz Racing School
800.849.7223
www.panozracingschool.com

PIAA
503.643.7422

Pioneer Electronics
310.952.2451
Jaed Arzadon

Powerdyne
661.723.2800
www.powerdyne.com

Power Slot Brakes
818.709.4800

Pro-Power
954.491.6988

Recaro
248.288.6800
www.recaro-neo.com

Rev Hard
818.764.4312
www.revhard.com

Richard Petty Driving Experience
800.237.3889

Rob Taylor Kustom Auto Graphics
619.698.1634
Rob Taylor

Santini Graphics
714.891.8895
Pete Santini

SCCA
303.694.7223
www.sccaproracing.com

SEMA
909.860.2961
www.sema.com
John Jeffries

Skunkworks
510.781.0538

Sony
201.930.7077

Sparco
714.444.4874
www.sparco.it

Sport Compact Car Magazine
714.939.2400
Larry Saavedra

Sprint Springs
909.484.1799
www.sprintsprings.com

Starbuck Graphics
909.735.6053
Doug Starbuck

Super Street Magazine
323.782.2322
Howard Lim
Matt Pearson

Suspension Techniques
559.266.9173
www.belltechcorp.com

TSW Alloy Wheels
949.609.0800
Bill Andrews
www.tswnet.com

Tipton Honda
889 Arnele Ave.
El Cajon, CA 92020
619.440.1000
Ty Tipton
www.tiptonhonda.com

Tokico Shocks
310.534.4934
Richard Meyer

Toucan Industries
203.265.5667

Toyo Tires
714.236.2080
www.toyo.com
Sheri McCullough

Turbo Engineering
303.271.3997

Turbonetics
805.529.8995
www.turbonetics.com
Oly Lysenstoen

Vision Entertainment
949.376.7942
Richard Goodwin

Vitek
770.663.7700
Steve Haywood

Wings West
949.722.9995
www.wingswest.com
Ernie Bunnell

Xenon
714.632.1709
www.teamxenon.com
Craig Way

XS Engineering
714.992.4133
www.xsengineering.com

Yokohama Tires
714.870.3800
www.yokohamatire.com
Mark Richter

INDEX

tinted/smoked light covers, 18, 107
Limited-slip differentials (LSD), 84
Linear springs, 24-25
Line-lock device, 95
Local clubs, 148-149
Lowback seats, 114
Lowering springs, 17, 25
Lowrider modifications, 13-14, 17-18

M

M & H, 21
Magazines, 21, 41
Magna Core ignition wires, 55
Magnesium wheels, 19
Mail order, 21
Manual transmission. *See* Shifter
Maximum Boost (Bell), 74
Mazda
    Miata, 7, 74, 76, 81-82
    RX2, 3
Miata Club of America (MCA), 148
Mickey Thompson, 21
Mid-Ohio School, 146
Motec ECU, 59
Murals paint style, 125-127

N

National clubs, 148, 149
Neuspeed, 29
Nissan, 3, 4
Nitrous oxide, 17, 76-79, 78
Nology, 55, 57, 77
NOPI Nationals, 116

O

Oil cavitation, 70
Oil pressure gauge, 120
Oil pump, 70
Organic metal clutch, 82-83
Overdrive pulleys, 17, 49

P

PaceSetter
    Exhaust, 5
    Quick-Shift unit, 85
Painting, 18, 123-129
    cost of, 128, 129
    heat paint, used in headers, 51

selecting a painter, 129
styles, 123-129
Panels paint style, 127
Panoz Racing School, 146
Peek, Gary, 25
Performance driving, 131-146
Performance springs, 17, 25-29
PIAA, 100
Pistons, 17, 70-71, 78
Pit area, autocross, 140
Polyurethane
    bushings, 17, 32, 85
    styling packages, 103
Powder-coated air induction systems, 45
Power Slot, 92
Powertrain, 72
Prelude
    engine, 62, 67-69
    transmission, 86
Progressive-rate springs, 24

Q

Quick-Shift unit, PaceSetter, 85

R

Racing seats, 18, 114-115
Reaction time, drag racing, 144
Rear brakes
    disc, 94
    drum, 89, 90, 94
Rear deck wings, 18, 97, 98, 104-106
Rear seats, 116
Rear valance, 18, 98, 101-102
Rear-wheel drive, 84, 95
Recaro, 115
Resources, 21, 78, 151-155
Retail stores, 21
Retainers, 71-72
Richard Petty Driving Experience, 146
Road adhesion, 104-105
Road racing. *See* Autocross
Rocker arms, 72
Rocker shafts, 72
Rods, 78
Rod-style shifting, 85
Roll bars, 18, 121
RS Akimoto, 45
Rubber bushings, 32

S

Alan Paradise

O ver the past 15 years, Alan Paradise has established himself as a leading automotive journalist. In 1987, he pioneered a new enthusiast's niche by developing a publication to speak to a new generation of performance enthusiasts. He defined this segment as "sport compact cars". This vision of the automotive future gave way to the highly successful magazine, which bears that name. Paradise is credited with creating and developing *Sport Compact Car* magazine, serving as its editor for the title's first four years. He has also served on the staffs of numerous other niche-market publications, including *Truckin'*, *MiniTruckin'*, *EuroSportCar*, and *Street Rodder*. Currently, he is the editor of *Miata Magazine*, *HCI Magazine*, *British Motoring*, *SpinOff* and *Celebrity Garages*. He is a longtime performance enthusiast, owning and building a wide range of cars from classics, muscle cars, street rods, sports cars to import performance cars.

PHOTO CREDITS

Cover

Front Cover photo by *Alan Paradise*.
Back Cover: top two photos courtesy *American Honda Motor Co.*
Back Cover: bottom two photos by *Alan Paradise*.
Back Cover fence photo courtesy of *Photodisc*.

Interior

All photographs in the interior of the book by *Alan Paradise*, with the exception of:

Tipton Honda: page 2, fig. 1-2
Eibach Springs: page 5, fig. 1-5, concept Civic
Lowrider Magazine: page 13, fig. 2-5
                              page 14, fig. 2-6
                              page 126, fig. 10-4